In the Shadow of the Great Charter

In the Shadow of the Great Charter

Common Law Constitutionalism and the Magna Carta

Robert M. Pallitto

University Press of Kansas

Published by the University Press of Kansas (Lawrence, Kansas 66045), which was organized by the Kansas Board of Regents and is operated and funded by Emporia State University, Fort Hays State University, Kansas State University, Pittsburg State University, the University of Kansas, and Wichita State University

Library of Congress Cataloging-in-Publication Data

Pallitto, Robert M., 1964– author.
In the shadow of the great charter : common law constitutionalism and the Magna Carta / Robert M. Pallitto.
pages cm
Includes bibliographical references and index.
ISBN 978-0-7006-2091-3 (cloth : alk. paper) — ISBN 978-0-7006-2092-0 (ebook)
1. Civil rights—United States—History. 2. Constitutional history—United States. 3. Magna Carta. 4. Law—United States. —English influences. I. Title.
KF4749.P35 2015
342.7302′4—dc23
2014045940

British Library Cataloguing-in-Publication Data is available.

Printed in the United States of America

10 9 8 7 6 5 4 3 2 1

The paper used in this publication is recycled and contains 30 percent postconsumer waste. It is acid free and meets the minimum requirements of the American National Standard for Permanence of Paper for Printed Library Materials Z39.48-1992.

For my parents,
Kathryn Motoviloff and Robert E. Pallitto

Contents

Acknowledgments

It has been tremendously enjoyable and gratifying to explore the Magna Carta's legacy in the United States, and the help and support given me by others have made the experience an especially good and valuable one. Charles Myers first encouraged me to pursue this project, and since then he has guided me through it expertly at every step. I owe him a great debt of thanks, and it has truly been a pleasure to work with him. Eric Kasper and the anonymous reviewers of the manuscript made many astute and constructive suggestions for improving it, and I am most grateful for their advice and feedback as well. Any errors, of course, are my own responsibility. This book had its genesis in a symposium-in-print on the meaning and legacy of the Magna Carta, which was edited by Kenton Worcester in 2010 for the journal *PS: Political Science and Politics*.

Many friends, family members, and colleagues provided support of one kind or another. In particular, I would like to thank (in no particular order) Ana Melendez, Larry Perfetti, Emily Bregman, Bob and Gwyn Murray, Ellen, Roger, and Andrew Miller, John and Kerry Motoviloff, Christina Pallitto, Ben Smith, Kathryn Motoviloff, Robert E. Pallitto, Jeff Hasler, Cheryl Hulteen, David Plotke, Patricia J. Williams, and Louis Fisher.

My friends and colleagues in Seton Hall's Department of Political Science and Public Affairs were always positive, supportive, and encouraging as I saw this project to completion. Special thanks to Wigeby Toussaint for encouragement and countless acts of helpfulness. I am extremely fortunate to work with such an exceptional group of people, and I hope they know how much I appreciate them.

This book was written during my sabbatical in 2013. I am most grateful to Seton Hall University for allowing me a break from normal teaching and service responsibilities so that I could immerse myself in English and American legal history. As any scholar knows, there is nothing more valuable than uninterrupted time to write.

My children, John, Daniel, and Isabel, bring me more happiness than I can describe here, and I thank them for simply being themselves. Finally, I want to thank Laura Melendez for being there to see me through another book, giving me confidence when I lacked it and love when I needed it. Her companionship is a constant joy.

1

Introduction

> Magna Carta has been preserved not as a museum piece, but as part of the common law of England, to be defended, maintained or repealed as the needs and function of the law required. That so much of what survives is now concerned with individual liberty is a reflexion of the quality of the original act of 1215. It was adaptable. This was its greatest and most important characteristic.
>
> J. C. Holt, *Magna Carta*

In a world drastically changed by the 9/11 attacks, Supreme Court justice Anthony Kennedy authored a 2008 legal opinion deciding whether "war on terror" detainees could be barred from U.S. courts. By military order and congressional act, the U.S. government had declared that these detainees, many of whom were confined at the Guantanamo Bay Naval Base, were not entitled to petition the federal courts for release from their confinement. Once they were determined to be properly classified as "enemy combatants," they would be tried before a military tribunal or simply detained indefinitely. The doors of the federal courts were closed to them.

The detainees claimed that stripping the courts of jurisdiction in this way was unlawful. They sought to file habeas corpus petitions in federal court, following a time-honored procedure in Anglo-American law by which prisoners challenge the government's authority to hold them. In the United States, habeas corpus is enshrined in constitutional text. The constitution requires that the writ of habeas corpus be available to prisoners at all times unless Congress explicitly suspends it and effectively declares martial law. Because there had been no formal suspension, the detainees reasoned, they were entitled to make habeas corpus petitions and could not be blocked from doing so.

Justice Kennedy agreed and ruled in the detainees' favor. His majority opinion linked the writ of habeas corpus to the U.S. Constitution, of course, but also to a much earlier document: the Magna Carta, or Great Charter, of AD 1215. For Kennedy, habeas corpus "became the means by which the promise of Magna Carta was fulfilled."[1] Among its numerous provisions setting forth rules for interactions between King John and the English nobility of the time, the Magna Carta declared in Article 39 that no one would be imprisoned except by the "law of the land." It was this provision that Kennedy took to contain the "promise" of liberty, a promise that had been redeemed in modernity by the emergence of habeas corpus as an accepted and regularly used form of pleading. He ascribed more than a symbolic significance to the 800-year-old document; he acknowledged its immediate practical effect on legal outcomes. The Constitution requires scrupulous protection of habeas corpus rights, and Kennedy traced that requirement back to the Magna Carta.

Why would the Supreme Court continue, today, to invoke an agreement between an English king and his barons that was made eight centuries ago—and to cite it as a source of individual rights and a limitation on government power? Why, especially, would it do so in the midst of a national security crisis brought on by the 2001 terror attacks? To address these specific questions is to probe the history of modern civil liberties, but it is also to explore the process by which judges go about deciding individual rights cases. First, though, some historical background on the Magna Carta itself is in order.

The Magna Carta's Origins

The Magna Carta was signed at Runnymede in June 1215. King John met an armed group of barons dressed for war in a meadow on the river Thames. The king gave his seal to the document, and it was signed by a group of barons who represented the rebellious faction. The signing/sealing of the Magna Carta concluded tense and protracted negotiations precipitated by complaints and disputes between the king and the barons regarding the king's use of power. In the course of the dispute, the rebel barons had taken control of London, and they were actually in possession of the city as they negotiated with the Crown. There is much historical evidence to establish a high level of tension and an imminent threat of violence in 1215 England. In addition to the physical occupation of London by the barons, there were letters of "safe conduct" issued to certain members of the nobility by King John in the weeks leading up to the June 19 ceremony at Runnymede. The king issued these letters so that the nobles could travel freely through the realm without fear of arrest or attack. The need for such documentation suggests a state of hostility between the warring groups. The barons sought guarantees of reform from the king in exchange for a promise that they would remain loyal to him.[2] About a week before the ceremonial acceptance of the Magna Carta at Runnymede, discussions between King John and the barons had produced a document that J. C. Holt calls the "Articles of the Barons."[3] A copy of this document was retained by Stephen Langton, the archbishop of Canterbury, who served as intermediary between the disputants, and it formed an agreement in principle indicating that progress in negotiations had taken place. The parties then made a "firm peace" at Runnymede on June 19, as the Articles of the Barons became the Magna Carta, and both sides agreed to be bound by its terms. Although a "firm peace" was reached on June 19 as the barons reestablished their loyalty to the king, the pacifying effect of the Charter did not last long. Two months later (after the immediate danger of war had passed), Pope Innocent III annulled it, claiming that the king had only agreed to its terms under duress. Following annulment, hostilities resumed. The Magna Carta was reinstated and reissued several times subsequently, most immediately in 1216, 1217, and 1225. The 1215 text is set forth in the appendix.

The Magna Carta of 1215 memorialized "concessions" made by King John to the barons. Its sixty-three articles cover a range of contested issues between the king and the people, including the following:

- rules for inheritance
- regulation of marriage
- debt collection
- court jurisdiction and procedures
- the proportionality of fines to offenses
- fair and just legal proceedings
- freedom of travel for merchants
- creation and use of "forests"[4]
- restoration of property seized by the Crown
- real property law

These concessions had to do with property rights as well as individual liberties. In fact, these categories overlap: for example, provisions of the Charter establish procedures and schedules for amercements (fines), which amount to deprivation of property but also concern liberty because they are penal in nature. Some of the property issues might appear quite mundane to us today (such as how to select sheriffs to oversee royal forests), but they were important and consequential to the parties involved. Other topics covered, such as the purchasing of marriage rights by one family from another, seem anachronistic to the modern reader, and yet their implications for individual liberty are obvious. At the root of many of the concessions wrought by the Magna Carta was the establishment of the rule of law: "It maintained the principle that authority was subject to law."[5] Because the king controlled the availability of legal process and determined what legal claims were cognizable and who could bring them, access to courts was a fundamental element of rule of law. By granting or withholding legal process, the king was mediating justice itself. Subjects expected and sometimes demanded that legal process be available to them.[6]

Kenton Worcester has pointed out that the substantive content of the Magna Carta was foreshadowed in an earlier document issued by King Henry I in 1100 at his coronation. In fact, the barons negotiating with King John in 1215 specifically sought as one of their demands confirmation of the earlier Charter of Henry I.[7] They sought to have Henry I's charter reaffirmed by King John. In the end, the Magna Carta "followed the pattern set by the Charter of Henry I in devoting its first section to the liberties of the Church. The next sections, as in Henry's charter, were concerned with the king's feudal rights. Magna Carta, like Henry's charter, represented an attempt to state the detailed implications of the oath to destroy evil and maintain just customs which kings swore at their coronation."[8] Although Henry did not use the "law of the land" phraseology, his coronation charter is similar in tone to the Magna Carta: it is conciliatory, and it delineates specific rights that members of the kingdom will enjoy as against the king. Like the Magna Carta, the Charter of Liberties of 1100 announces certain procedures that will be followed regarding marriage, baronial service, collection of debts, and other matters.[9] Thus, the barons in 1215 were invoking "custom and precedent" by linking their demands with earlier promises made by a long-dead king.[10] Just as the Magna Carta serves as evidence of legal limits on executive power for modern commentators, so did Henry I's charter stand for limits on royal power as the barons cited it in 1215. Even more than the specific terms, the *act* of promising publicly to rule justly and to "destroy evil" was difficult to rescind. King John tried to do so as he moved his army north later in the year and resumed a state of war with the barons, but his concessions helped to solidify the notion that kings were constrained by law. As Holt puts it, "Where it concerned justice the Charter asserted broad principles which had their roots deep in the past."[11]

Magna Carta's Legacy in the United States

Throughout the more than 200 years the Supreme Court has been in existence, the record of its decisional law shows the continuing influence of Magna Carta principles. Due process (in criminal proceedings) and habeas corpus are the best known of the principles for which the Magna Carta is cited, and they are the ones that receive the vast majority of attention in this book. Nonetheless, the Court has cited other Magna Carta provisions in a variety of legal disputes. References to the Magna Carta in Supreme Court case law are frequent. Even if passing and extraneous references are excluded, more than a hundred citations by the Supreme Court can still be found.[12] The following is a sampling of decisions citing lesser-known provisions of the Great Charter:

- *The Nereide* (1815)[13] (safekeeping of merchants' goods during war—Article 41)
- *South v. Maryland* (1855)[14] (limitations on powers of a sheriff—Article 45)
- *Kent v. Dulles* (1958)[15] (right to travel—Article 42)

- *Trop v. Dulles* (1958)[16] (revocation of citizenship offends "dignity of man"—Articles 39, 40)
- *Klopfer v. North Carolina* (1966)[17] (the right to a speedy trial—Article 40)
- *U.S. v. Mara* (1973)[18] (right to grand jury finding—Articles 39, 40)
- *Solem v. Helm* (1983)[19] (proportionality of punishments to offenses—Article 20)
- *Browning-Ferris Industries v. Kelco Disposal* (1989)[20] (limitations on fines or damages —Articles 20, 21)
- *Idaho v. Coeur d'Alene Tribe* (1997)[21] (ownership and use of navigable waters—Article 33)
- *Duryea v. Guarneri* (2011)[22] (right to petition the government regarding grievances—Article 61)
- *Hosanna Tabor Evangelical Lutheran Church v. Equal Employment Opportunity Commission* (2012)[23] (religious freedom—Articles 1, 63)

These citations span the entire history of the United States, and they continue up to the present. In chapter 2, I will show how even the colonial charters reflected the influence of the Magna Carta as colonists claimed certain liberties against the king just as the people in England did. But as the Charter was referenced in Supreme Court decisions it became influential in the development of the constitutional common law.

The Practice of Judicial Interpretation

It is a convention, and perhaps an inevitable obligation, for judges to set forth the grounds on which their decisions are based. This practice safeguards the legitimacy of the court as a public institution and also lends persuasive weight to decisions that stand as precedent to be scrutinized by later courts. It has been clear, at least since *Marbury v. Madison* was decided in 1803, that judges would regularly cite constitutional text as authority for judicial decisions. And so as judges decide cases (particularly cases involving the limits of state power over individuals), they must construe constitutional provisions such as the Bill of Rights and the institutional grants of power found in Articles I and II. No matter how clear and unambiguous those provisions might appear to the outside observer, there is always room for questions and disagreement among the ultimate arbiters of constitutional meaning who sit on the Supreme Court. One need only compare majority and dissenting opinions in the same case in order to see how sharply different the justices' interpretive approaches can be. Moreover, many justices have over time spoken publicly about their individual approaches to the work of constitutional interpretation, and so we have a record in the justices' own words indicating how they go about it. Sometimes there is more than one answer to an interpretive dispute. And sometimes the plain meaning yields a result that is unacceptable or even absurd. Akhil Amar notes that the text of Article I, Section 3 would seem to allow the vice president, as president pro tempore of the Senate, to preside over his own trial on impeachment charges.[24] Of course, such an arrangement would make no sense. Amar's point here is that the written text does not answer all of the questions that arise in the course of disputes over governing. The Constitution cannot be read in isolation from principles and commitments predating the document itself, he argues, and in a general sense this is true whether one adheres to an "original meaning" approach, a "living constitution" approach, or any other methodology of interpretation.

Amar suggests that an "unwritten constitution" exists alongside the written document. In addition to rules rooted in the common law, the unwritten constitution draws on principles of modern political thought and certain documents generated through American history that reflect those principles. Amar includes the Gettysburg Address, the opinion in *Brown v. Board of Education*, and the Reverend Martin Luther King Jr.'s "I Have a Dream" speech in his list of the texts that help to form the unwritten constitution.[25] Of course, once the reader moves outside the text to search for interpretive guidance, the problem of what to include arises. In other words, what counts as part of the unwritten constitution, and how do particular elements (a speech, an interpretive principle) represent more than idiosyncratic choices? How can one say that they stand for things that everyone would choose as constitutive? As Amar himself poses the question, "Exactly what sorts of things outside the text are sensibly viewed as genuinely 'constitutional' things?"[26]

Another way of posing this problem is to say that iconic statements like the *Brown* opinion and the Declaration of Independence all conform to some ideal, some core commitment, such as the "liberal tradition," as Louis Hartz suggested.[27] In other words, we can say that they are not random choices because they fit with something that we have already identified. But what is the warrant for *that* principle? How do we identify it? How do we define it? Why should my vision of that commitment be taken as more authoritative than yours?

Constitutionalism

The question of what binds legal actors beyond constitutional text has of course been addressed by many commentators. The concept of constitutionalism is a connecting thread through much of this literature. At the most general level, constitutionalism simply suggests that the constitutional text binds and constrains legal actors, generating a politics that is more than just the play of power. There are commitments that are regularly honored and rules that are followed, and these rules are assented to and considered binding because participants in public disputes view them as legitimate. Specific versions of constitutionalism include "common law constitutionalism," a school of thought that holds "that courts do and should develop the meaning of general or ambiguous constitutional texts by reference to tradition and precedent, rather than to original understanding."[28] For example, Amar resolves the previously mentioned quandary about vice presidential impeachment by using a long-accepted legal maxim that is so widely honored, he says, that it "goes without saying."[29] So if the text of Article I seems to permit the vice president to preside over his own impeachment proceedings, and we can see that such a reading would be absurd, we can resolve the conflict between the written text and common sense by invoking the rule that "no one shall be judge in his [*sic*] own cause." Following that maxim, the vice president would be prohibited from presiding over his own trial. The maxim is not part of the text, but it is part of a tradition of legal dispute resolution long followed by judges and common law commentators alike. In fact, James Madison makes reference to it in *The Federalist* No. 10.

Critiques of Common Law Constitutionalism

As intuitively appealing and cogent as this version of constitutionalism might sound, it has troubled some scholars. Frank Michelman, for example, worries that Supreme Court justices practicing common law constitutionalism will often find themselves caught between procedural and substantive notions of democracy.[30] As they perform their roles in a democratic system, they may imagine democracy as purely procedural (i.e., as a set of rules that must be followed) or as a substantive state of being that is ideal for individuals. Michelman sees this conflict exemplified most clearly in the life and work of Justice William Brennan. Deeply committed to unfettered and universal democracy, Brennan nonetheless saw the need to protect individuals' liberty and dignity from government, and that obligation often led him to rule contrary to the expressed preference of the majority of the citizenry. In other words, Brennan believed that a *procedural* democracy of rules guaranteeing access to the process of self-government stood alongside—and in tension with—a *substantive* notion of democracy as the highest aspiration of human development, which required protection and nurturing that often had to come from the courts. This tension troubled Michelman because judges holding a substantive conception of democracy (like Brennan) must necessarily refer to "laws of lawmaking" that would help them to evaluate majority enactments and see whether those enactments tended to advance or threaten their substantive conception. And, of course, the problem of process arises at this higher level as well: if the "laws of lawmaking" are not democratically enacted, the problem of justifying them arises. Once a judge rests a particular decision on a higher commitment such as the essential dignity of all humans qua humans, that judge has violated the procedural conception of democracy because popular sovereignty has neither enacted nor authorized that higher principle. Michelman did not think Justice Brennan ever resolved this tension, though Brennan "gave us the best exhibition of his version of democracy that we and our posterity are ever likely to see."[31]

Adrian Vermeule posits common law constitutionalism as the opposite methodological pole to originalism. Judges can gravitate to one pole and use the original meaning of constitutional text as their guide in construing that text, or they can go to the other pole and look outside the text and rely on precedent or tradition. Original meaning has been explained by Justice Scalia —one of the most forceful proponents of the approach—as "the fair meaning of the word," "the ordinary meaning of the words in their context," and "a persuasive indication of what the Constitution meant to the people at the time."[32] This approach is bound by the text and only looks beyond the text insofar as to determine the meaning of its terms, and not for any other interpretive guidance. Common law constitutionalism, by contrast, as I have shown, allows precedent and tradition to influence interpretation of the text when questions arise. The extratextual sources can be seen as superior, sometimes, to the text standing alone.

Vermeule is skeptical of the argument that common law constitutionalism allows judges to access "latent wisdom" and is therefore superior.[33] He questions the *epistemic* version of the constitutionalists' claim by pointing out that legislatures are arguably better at producing fully informed legal texts than judges are. Simply put, there are far more legislators and legislative staffers than there are Supreme Court justices, and as a result the legislators have access to greater informational resources, which should in turn generate better outputs. Why, then, assume that judges' decisions reached in reliance on precedent and tradition are more likely to embody latent wisdom than legislative enactments are? Second, Vermeule considers whether common law constitutionalism might be more defensible in *evolutionary* terms than epistemic terms, and once again he decides that it is not. He sees no basis for concluding that constitutional decisions tend over time to evolve toward optimal results. Isolating a mechanism within the process of adjudication that would cause this result is confounding, for that mechanism would have to operate at a level above human intention to "cause[ ] the uncoordinated action of biased judges to produce a body of common law that is economically efficient."[34] In other words, the "heritability" (in evolutionary biology terms) of superior principles must be explained by some force within the legal system, such as the tendency of litigants to attack bad precedent and have it overruled. But judges have a range of options besides simply overruling bad precedent (refuse to hear the appeal, decline to reach the merits of the dispute, defer to stare decisis), and this is one reason why Vermeule rejects the evolutionary claim: common law cannot consistently evolve when judges have so many different options for disposing of a case. Also, gauging the value of constitutional decisions by "efficiency" is problematic to begin with. Many judges would resist the notion that "efficiency," rather than "justice" or "liberty," is the proper evaluative criterion for their rulings. A metric for judging the evolutionary progress of constitutional doctrine remains elusive.

Magna Carta, Tradition, and Constitutionalism

How, then, does the Magna Carta fit within current constitutional interpretive practice, and how did it come to occupy that place? Frederick Gedicks has shown that the path from the Magna Carta's signing to its place in twenty-first-century American constitutional interpretation is not an entirely straight one. In the political thought of eighteenth-century England, we encounter a fork in the road. The Magna Carta set out limitations on state power, which initially meant the power of a monarch. Over time, as the institution of Parliament became part of English government, the guarantee of individual liberty in the Magna Carta became applicable against Parliament as well.[35] In the eighteenth century, however, a new understanding of the relationship among legislature, executive, and the people took shape, in which the "supremacy of Magna Carta, due process, and the common law, in which Coke had placed so much faith, was replaced by the supremacy of Parliament."[36] Gedicks continues: "This new understanding held the English constitution to be what Parliament chose to enact or repeal as law, even when such actions violated natural or common law."[37] In this arrangement of state power, the legislature (Parliament) constrains the executive, but the people possess no such check on the power of Parliament. When the U.S. Constitution was adopted later in the eighteenth century, the American experience proceeded differently, through the instantiation of the practice of judicial review. Judges say "what the law is" in the context of disputes over constitutional meaning, and so judicial power counterbalances legislative decisions. To choose otherwise would be to equate the "law of the land" (in Article 39 terms) with whatever the legislature decided, thus foreclosing the application of any higher principle of justice. That path takes us to legal positivism, of course, and we must remember that that strain exists—indeed, must exist—in a democracy. Thus, to say that American law has proceeded according to constitutional rather than legislative supremacy is accurate only to the extent that the Supreme Court and the inferior courts have claimed the power for themselves to have the last word in disputes over constitutional meaning.

Current controversies over same-sex marriage implicate questions of constitutionalism and the balance between popular sovereignty and individual rights. When the Supreme Court invalidated the Defense of Marriage Act in 2013, it relied on a conception of individual liberty that is derived from constitutional jurisprudence but not stated explicitly in the constitutional text. Common law constitutionalism trumped the will of the legislature. As a result of the ruling, federal law could no longer define "marriage" in exclusively heterosexual terms. Because the decision pertained to a federal law, it pushed the conflict down to the states, which could still legislate on this issue. The states would become the only battleground where the same-sex marriage conflict would play out. In New Jersey, Governor Chris Christie suggested that the matter be put to the people directly, in the form of a public question. While this was a politically shrewd suggestion that allowed the governor to avoid taking sides on an emotionally freighted controversy during an election year, it also highlighted the tension between majority decision making and constitutional tradition. In response to the governor's suggestion, one legislative leader demurred, saying that civil rights should not be determined by majority vote.[38] This exchange illustrates two contrasting approaches to settling rights conflicts and also reminds us that the tension between the two approaches manifests itself in the most divisive conflicts of our time.

Habeas Corpus, Rule of Law, and Emergency Powers

Another contemporary dispute reflects the Magna Carta lineage as well: the question of emergency powers of the executive. This is not a new problem, of course, but the terror attacks of 9/11 have brought it to prominence in popular discourse as well as public law scholarship. When emergencies arise—particularly those that threaten the very existence of the state itself—the executive predictably seeks to exercise powers beyond those normally employed. For instance, the executive may seek to confine enemies of the state without criminal charges, to interrogate them aggressively, or to curtail due process rights in the trial context. One response to this dilemma was offered by the political theorist Carl Schmitt long ago: the executive must create a space for emergency action outside the law, a state of exception. There is a danger in creating such a "legal black hole," or "space beyond law," as David Dyzenhaus puts it.[39] If the executive gets to determine whether and when the rule of law will apply to it, then the rule of law ceases to function. Or, as Justice Kennedy put it, the test for applying the Constitution "must not be subject to manipulation by those whose power it is designed to restrain."[40] The possibility of a state of exception negates meaningful constraint on state power. But Dyzenhaus sees an equal or greater danger in what he calls "grey holes": where rule of law *may* apply, or applies to a limited extent.[41] These holes actually make it seem possible that law and exception can coexist, which is damaging to political theory and practice in the long run. At least Schmitt's approach has the virtue of eschewing all pretense that rule of law applies. Bruce Ackerman's "emergency constitution" is one theory that Dyzenhaus faults for suggesting that law continues to function when ordinary politics have been suspended. Ackerman suggests that an "emergency constitution" kicks in when certain threats arise, and that it must be authorized and reauthorized by ever-increasing legislative supermajorities.[42] But this "grey hole" makes the cessation of law difficult to see, as it covers up lawlessness with a veneer of legality.[43]

The "state of exception" shares one feature with common law constitutionalism. Both theories require us to look outside the text for guidance in resolving legal disputes. But it is a limited similarity. In the former case, the executive is free to take any action that is judged to be beneficial to the survival of the state. In the latter case, by contrast, judges are bound by limits of tradition and precedent, even if those limits admit of some ambiguity. Because of the extratextual aspect of the state of exception, though, it is an important area to explore in a study of constitutional tradition and rule of law.

The Magna Carta as Myth

For at least a century, scholars have written of a "myth of Magna Carta," suggesting that what the document actually meant to its signatories and the circumstances under which it was executed were quite different from what is commonly supposed. In an influential article from 1904, Edward Jenks argued that the Magna Carta had not been intended to establish liberties on behalf of the general citizenry but rather for the nobility alone.[44] The notion that modern liberty is coeval with the 1215 signing of the Magna Carta was, for Jenks, a fiction contradicted by historical circumstances. Jenks does not find evidence of baronial solicitude for the interests or concerns of the general population. He suggests that the majority of the English populace was unconcerned and uninvolved in the struggle between the nobility and the Crown. Moreover, Jenks contends that the "law of the land" provision of Article 39, which is most significant in American constitutional law, was meant to refer to nobility alone rather than to all the people. Article 39, he writes, "was no magnificent declaration of the rights of the common man; it was simply a recognition of the privileges of an aristocratic class, a class of landowners who, though not technically 'feudal,' can no more be ranked amongst 'the people,' than can the country gentleman of to-day."[45] Jenks places primary responsibility for this "myth" of Magna Carta as a populist victory on Sir Edward Coke. Jenks says that Coke's reading of the history of 1215 was political: he wanted to claim historical precedent for popular activism and use it in his own epoch: the "troublous times" preceding the English Civil War.[46] As he tried to make the Magna Carta a rallying point for popular resistance to the government, Coke cast it as a foundational source of individual liberty that all English citizens could claim as their heritage.

There is much truth to Jenks's view of Magna Carta as a myth. For one thing, habeas corpus probably predates the document by at least a decade, so it is not true that the Magna Carta gave birth to habeas corpus.[47] Also, most of the articles in the document pertain to specific aspects of the relationship between the Crown and the nobility. Two articles (6 and 8) regulate marriage, and two others (10 and 11) refer to "borrow[ing] . . . money from Jews" and "owing money to Jews," respectively. These four provisions hardly support a belief in the Magna Carta as a fountain of liberty. Moreover, King John renounced the Charter once the most acute danger prompting its issuance had passed. And, as Jenks points out, the fact that the Magna Carta was reissued repeatedly undercuts the claim that it was widely understood as the unshakable foundation of individual rights—why, Jenks asks, did reformers and royalists alike call for its reissuance time and again if it was already established as a binding source of rights protections?[48] In short, there is ample evidence to conclude that there is a mythical element to the narrative of the birth of modern liberty beginning with the Magna Carta.

At the same time, though, this mythical element can be overstated. The text of the Magna Carta refers to various categories of persons recognized within the social milieu of the time: landowners, debtors, widows, "freemen," clergy, merchants, criminal defendants, and civil litigants, among others. The reader cannot ignore these pluralistic references even if the political conditions surrounding the document's execution were far less democratic than a casual reading might suggest. Also, succeeding versions of the Magna Carta broadened its coverage so that it applied beyond the members of the nobility:

- Article 63 of the 1215 Charter granted liberties to "men in our kingdom."
- Article 2 of the 1216 Charter addressed "all the free men of our kingdom."
- The Preamble of the 1225 Charter applied to "all of our kingdom."

How much does it matter that there is a mythical element to the story of the Magna Carta? It is certainly important to recognize the actual historical circumstances surrounding the creation and execution of the Magna Carta. Rigorous historical inquiry serves to show that mythologies traceable to founding acts or moments persist—and operate similarly—in the development of different nations. It would be a mistake to ignore the facts of the Magna Carta's origin just as it would be misguided to ignore, say, the common class interests of many eighteenth-century American revolutionaries. At the same time, though, tradition gathers a force over time that is not dependent on the accuracy of its historical claims. The words and actions of Edward Coke, William Penn, and others who used the Magna Carta symbolically to further the cause of liberty strengthened the linkage between the document and the common law constitutionalist tradition. Their actions were arguably even more important to the tradition's development than the circumstances by which the Magna Carta came to be written and signed centuries earlier. Also, the provisions of the Magna Carta can be read as aspirations to a more inclusive rights tradition that would develop later, surpassing the narrow class boundaries of the parties to the original agreement. Akhil Amar makes a similar point about the Preamble to the U.S. Constitution. Amar notes that when the Preamble was written, "we the people" excluded slaves, women, and Native Americans. And yet the Preamble stated a promise of inclusion, according to Amar, that was eventually redeemed by a wider range of Americans. As he put it, the Preamble was like a portal through which those previously excluded groups would eventually pass.[49] Something similar could be said about the Magna Carta. Even if it initially protected only the nobility, its insistence that the government follow the "law of the land" would eventually benefit everyone who faced adverse government action, regardless of social standing. Viewed that way, it is far more than myth.

The best defense of the Magna Carta's central place in our legal tradition is a historical-pragmatic one. We can disagree over the original understanding of the Charter's terms among its signatories, and even over the meaning of "due process" among the founders of the Republic. What is clear, however, is the linkage between the Charter and habeas corpus that has strengthened over time, and the resulting linkage between habeas corpus and the rule of law. Compelling voices such as Edward Coke and William Brennan emphasized the importance of these connections, and in Brennan's case his practices of constitutional interpretation in the context of solving actual disputes have added weight to the tradition. To abandon the commitment to this principle with its warrant in historical experience would bring grave consequences that we have thus far avoided. Common law constitutionalism, with its lineage to the Magna Carta, has worked to produce a constitutional tradition that has proved workable and enduring. Rights gain meaning through the testing process of legal disputes, and the understandings that have developed up to this point are worth retaining.

Outline of the Book

This book will explore the influence of the Magna Carta on the contemporary jurisprudence of individual rights. To investigate this question, I will focus on specific areas of dispute and controversy located at particular historical moments in the nation's history. First, I will discuss the influence of the Magna Carta on legal thought in the North American colonies. I will also provide some insight into the English legal thought of the time concerning the Magna Carta. Next, I will examine pre–Civil War cases addressing the question of slavery. Here, while the courts in cases such as *State v. Mann* and *Dred Scott v. Sandford* were aware of the tradition by which Anglo-American law professed solicitude for individual liberty, they declared themselves helpless to intervene in the unequal power relationships between slaveholders and slaves. In one sense, this time period and the cases generated within it mark off a limit of courts' willingness to view the liberty-protecting tradition of the Magna Carta as a binding constraint on individual property rights.

Next, I will consider a development whose connection to the Magna Carta is not explicit: the change in the status of federal common law around the pivotal decision in *Erie Railroad v. Tompkins* (1938). Supreme Court justice Louis Brandeis's opinion in that case struck a new balance among state and federal courts and legislatures by declaring that there is no general federal common law. In other words, federal judges must follow the case law resulting from the decisions of state courts rather than generating precedents of their own in areas such as tort and insurance law. *Erie* had implications for constitutional theory in a number of ways. It relied on a particular view of the constitutional authority of the federal courts, and it "symbolized . . . the decline of customary, historical and natural rights jurisprudence and the rise of positivism and legal realism."[50] And because of its connection with the Legal Realist movement of the time, *Erie* also provides the opportunity to consider that important movement and its effect on legal thought in general in individual rights jurisprudence in particular. Thus, a chapter on federal common law in the early twentieth century becomes an important part of the story of common law constitutionalism and the Magna Carta.

Following that, I will discuss the "rights revolution" of the Warren Court as an instance where political and historical events gave shape to the tradition of rule of law and respect for individual rights. The general public is more familiar with the Court's landmark rulings on segregation, criminal defendants' rights, and other freedoms by virtue of their *substantive* content. However, those rulings are also important for my purposes here by virtue of their role in incorporating Bill of Rights guarantees so that they apply against the states as well as the federal government.

Then, I will consider the curtailment of habeas corpus by the Rehnquist Court. The decisions of this period raise the obvious question of the depth of commitment—on the part of the Supreme Court, at least—to the principle of habeas corpus. While the writ was not repudiated (this would have flown directly in the face of the constitutional text), it became more difficult to access. How did the Rehnquist Court address the long-standing commitment to habeas corpus as a pillar of individual liberty? What, if anything, has happened since the Rehnquist era that would restore the place of habeas corpus in the law of detention?

Finally, I will discuss the most recent context in which individual liberty as against the state has been contested: claims of heightened and even unreviewable executive power arising post-9/11 as the Bush and Obama administrations conducted the war on terror. Through my examination of these historical conflicts, I will consider the extent to which the Magna Carta's Article 39, with its "law of the land" guarantee, has functioned within American constitutionalism. The primary lessons to be learned here, I will argue, have to do with the way in which ideas come in conflict with power relations. On the one hand, the rule of law protected by Article 39 has been challenged and even threatened by the demands of power at certain crucial junctures. On the other hand, decisional law produced from these moments of conflict can—sometimes, though not always—actually strengthen commitments to liberty, thereby reinforcing the Magna Carta's declaration of liberty from state domination. In other words, in order to understand how we got from the Magna Carta's execution in 1215 to its use as a source of authority in 2008, we must examine closely the moments in U.S. history when attempts to preserve or increase power called the guarantee of individual liberty into question.

Let me add a word about the organization of this book. While it follows a broad chronological outline, some cross-referencing and forward/backward-looking is not only helpful but probably inevitable. One cannot properly analyze *Erie* without discussing *Swift v. Tyson* (1842), which *Erie* overruled. Similarly, in considering the tension between Magna Carta's conception of liberty and the pro-slavery rulings by American courts, comparison with substantive liberties as pronounced in later decisions is useful. And the Rehnquist Court's restriction of habeas corpus is best understood against the background of two preceding centuries of American habeas corpus jurisprudence. I hope that readers will find these occasional deviations from strict chronological narrative to be far more enlightening than distracting.

2

Early Theoretical Foundations

THE COMMON LAW MIND

Magna Carta is such a fellow, that he will have no sovereign.
Sir Edward Coke, quoted in Holt, *Magna Carta*

Common law constitutionalism as it is discussed today looks back to its English origins: both in the work of early commentators and in the judicative practices of the English courts.[1] In the person of Sir Edward Coke we have both, as he expounded on the sources and principles of common law reasoning while sitting on the bench and judging actual cases. Coke, who lived from 1552 to 1634, enjoyed a long and brilliant career as a politician, judge, and scholar, serving at various times as Speaker of the House of Commons, attorney general, and chief justice of the Court of Common Pleas and the King's Bench. As a justice, he challenged the actions of Parliament for being violative of the common law. He wrote a highly influential treatise entitled *The Institutes of the Law of England*, which was cited widely in England and later in the United States. Coke provides a key link between the Magna Carta and American constitutionalism by virtue of his dual role as commentator and practitioner; he participates in the story as he tells it. And the story moves forward by the persistent recurrence of two questions: First, how can judges ascertain the meaning of statutory terms? Second, where should they look for guidance when those terms fail to provide a clear answer to the question submitted to them for decision, or when there is a clear answer but it conflicts with a claim of right? Of course, "statute" here bears a similarity to constitutional text in that both are written law, though it will be necessary to differentiate statute and constitution at many points in the following discussion.

The term "positive law," which I will use interchangeably with "statutory law," denotes written rules created (or *posited*) by the sovereign that carry the force of law. In Hobbesian terms, this would include the pronouncements of the sovereign; modern readers would understand it to be the enactments of the legislature in a representative democracy. In both cases, the body of positive law comes to bear on individual disputants standing before a court. One side in the dispute seeks the benefit of the statute's terms, while the opposing party urges a different construction of the statute, or perhaps even argues that the statutory rule does not cover the case at all. Judges are required by their role in government to resolve disputes, and in the process of resolving disputes they cannot avoid interpreting rules because "what statutes themselves mean for a case requires interpretation."[2] Thus, the law made by judges (common law) and the law made by legislative acts (positive law) are distinct forms existing in tension with one another. Common law is "law seen from the point of view of a judge faced with a controversy," while statutory law is seen from "the point of view of a sovereign monarch faced with an unmanageable people, or a sovereign people faced with civil war."[3] So these two lawmaking enterprises differ in terms of viewpoint, but the tension between them stems in part from their shared reliance on written law in the form of constitutional text. Even before there was a U.S. Constitution, there was the Magna Carta, and judges have long had a "habit of declaring fundamental law in written documents."[4] Stoner provides evidence of Sir Edward Coke treating the Magna Carta in just that way. The primacy of constitutional text over statutory text flows not only from the supremacy claims expressed within the document itself but also from the belief that the document invoked and reflected "fundamental law." Common law constitutionalism, then, relies on written law but seeks to discern within it truths that precede each written expression of law. But what are those truths? What is their foundation? How do judges recognize them?

Forms of Reason

At first glance, it looks as though *reason* is the key ingredient that allows judges to discern and apply fundamental law—that fundamental legal truths are grounded in reason, and that reasoning is the process through which they are discovered and applied. However, a number of complications arise. Duncan Kennedy reminds us that reason as a *source* of rights is distinct from reason as a *means* for specifying rights: the former tells us where rights come from while the latter tells us what they mean.[5] It may be that the ground of rights is not accessible to all who might inquire about them—special training, wisdom, or perspective might be necessary in order to perceive the content of fundamental rights. Or perhaps other considerations intervene in the process of judging actual cases, so that the objectively correct rights principle must be balanced with justice and fairness to produce the optimal outcome. Turning to Coke's commentary on the common law, we see that for him, reason is linked closely with the common law, but it is a particular conception of reason that Coke offers. As Stoner describes this conception:

> Reason is not original and comprehensive; rather, it takes what is given and works upon it, improves it. It does this

> by bringing to bear not logic alone, but logic together with wide learning. The reason Coke appealed to is not a theoretical but a practical faculty. It is certainly not mere discretion, but neither is it logic devoid of experience. It is a trained way of thinking, not arbitrary but also not apodictic.[6]

Coke's treatment of the Magna Carta is consistent with this conception of reason. He celebrates its importance in the development of English law—indeed, his name frequently appears in discussions of the Magna Carta's legacy among scholars as well as in popular contexts—and he interprets Article 39 of the Magna Carta broadly, as fundamental law. In the Article 39 requirement that the king must follow "the law of the land," we see an example of a written rule calling for explication. What "law" does this phrase signify? It seems that the common law is the likely reference, so that the "law of the land" includes the artifacts of custom and precedent that compose the common law. According to Coke, the wise and learned judge would determine what parts of that past learning to preserve and apply. And so the common law develops over time. He noted that many minds contributed to this body of law over years and decades, so that the accumulated knowledge surpassed the capability that one judge alone would have when asked to solve legal problems. When Coke opined about possible changes in statutory law that Parliament sought to make, he warned of the dangers of departing from or abandoning the accretion of knowledge produced by the work of common law judges through the years.

Sir Edward Coke and Doctor Bonham's Case

Coke's conception of reason in the common law can be seen in his opinion in *Doctor Bonham's Case* (1610)—perhaps the most famous and consequential legal opinion he wrote. Bonham was imprisoned for practicing medicine without a license, in violation of a statute regulating the medical profession. He urged a different reading of the statute, suggesting that a physician gained the right to practice medicine either through a license *or* upon graduating from university, as Bonham himself had done. Bonham's reading prevailed. Coke's opinion was one among several in *Bonham's Case*, but it became the most consequential by far. Bonham had not been accused of malpractice but merely of practicing without a license, and so the majority holding was that the college lacked the power to discipline him, as its grant of power allowed only regulation of malpractice. In ruling for Bonham, Coke chose between two readings of the written rule, and he favored the one that restrained collective power and protected the individual. Thus, the application of a common law rule functioned as a limitation on state power. As in all subsequent instances of judicial review, the importance of the case as precedent extended beyond the interests of the individual litigant who benefited from the decision. So as the judge (Coke) chooses among alternative decisional grounds, we must assume he is aware of the larger legal and political significance of the outcome. It is interesting to note how Coke makes his choice. The regulatory body here was the London College of Physicians. The college granted medical licenses and also collected the fines levied against unlicensed practitioners such as Bonham. The authority to license and punish had been granted by the Crown and affirmed by Parliament. However, this dual role meant that the college was acting as *judge in its own cause*,[7] determining to impose a punishment that would enrich the college itself. Such an arrangement deprived Bonham of a fair proceeding.

Again, the significance of *Doctor Bonham's Case* reaches beyond the interests of the parties involved. Gedicks sees this ruling as a foundational moment in the history of due process generally and of substantive due process in particular: "Coke was trying to give content to the law's restraint on power; that is, he was trying to give substance to due process. There were, he thought, things that the supreme power in the state, even the king in Parliament, could not lawfully do, no matter how hard he tried."[8] This is a bold reading but a fair one. Coke voted to void an action —imprisoning Bonham—that had been duly authorized by law. The "law of the land" to which Coke appealed was superior, or "higher," than the Royal Order and Parliamentary acts that the College of Physicians relied on.[9]

It is but a small step from this articulation of judicial review (as we would call it, looking back on the case from a twenty-first-century vantage point) as a limit on state power to the birth of judicial review by the U.S. Supreme Court in *Marbury v. Madison* and subsequently.[10] Edward Corwin's important commentary, entitled "The 'Higher Law' Background of American Constitutional Law" (1928), helped to remind American audiences of the English common law roots of judicial review.[11] Corwin argued that Sir Edward Coke influenced the founders of the American republic as they designed a structure for their new government, and that Coke's teaching led them eventually to instantiate the practice of judicial review. Corwin's lengthy two-part article on the topic has been cited widely since it first appeared in print nearly a century ago. Largely because of Corwin's work, it has become conventional wisdom among legal historians and theorists of constitutional jurisprudence that American judicial review sprang directly from Coke's famous opinion in *Bonham's Case*.

However, Gary McDowell has argued that this influence is overstated. He finds no mention of Coke's work in many places we would expect it to appear: the federal Constitutional Convention, the state ratifying conventions, Hamilton's contributions to *The Federalist*, or *Marbury v. Madison*. McDowell suggests that the importance of higher law constitutionalism (which Corwin defines as the practice of judicial review guided by sources outside the constitutional text, particularly natural law) actually developed as a *result* of Corwin's influence. As McDowell puts it, "The influence of Bonham's case came from within the scholarly world; its significance stems not from history but from the historians."[12] A current of thought moving within the insular world of the legal academy is quite a different thing from an idea that motivates practitioners of statecraft and generates institutional principles by which the government of a new nation is run. But even if a clear line of influence from Coke to Jefferson or John Marshall cannot be traced, we must acknowledge at least the possibility that Corwin's work influenced judges practicing judicial review *after* his claims about "higher law constitutionalism" became known. Supreme Court opinions frequently cite legal scholarship; the opinions discussed in this book will provide ample proof of that fact. It may be that Corwin's contribution was to revive a set of ideas from an earlier time by articulating them in a way that fit with the social conditions and judicial practices of the early twentieth century. And nearly a century later, Corwin "continues to inform and shape the bulk of contemporary constitutional scholarship."[13]

McDowell's second criticism of Corwin is more devastating. It has to do with terminological and conceptual confusion. He charges that Corwin tends to use the terms "common law," "higher law," and "natural law" interchangeably, when in fact they have different meanings. Common law and natural law are distinct concepts. Because common law judges look to tradition and precedent for guidance in deciding cases, they may invoke rights that are coeval with the human condition (natural rights). In doing so, they draw upon natural law. But it is also the case quite often that common law relies on maxims, or rules of construction, that are independent of natural law. Coke's decisional ground in *Bonham's Case* (that no one should be "judge in his own cause") is an example of a maxim grounding legal interpretation. Thus, common law can be, but need not be, reliant on natural law.

Similarly, "higher law" and "natural law" bear distinct meanings. "Higher law" is sometimes used synonymously with "common law," but the same problem arises. "Higher law" refers to principles that trump statutory text. In other words, there is something more fundamental than the written law, something with a superior claim to authority, that overrides the law enacted by the legislature. "Higher law" rests on a trumping principle, but the trumping principle need not be based in natural law.[14] "Natural law" claims a specific basis for a law's validity: there is some incontestable ground for the truth of a claim, some first cause that cannot be questioned. For example, consider the principle that people owe kindness to one another. If I ground that principle by saying that God commands us to be kind to one another, I am appealing to natural law. This commandment is valid because it proceeds from God. There is no prior cause preceding the word of God to which the commandment can be linked. Once again, though, higher law can be reliant on natural law, but it need not be. Higher law may pertain to other things: it may be seen as justice as fairness, or it may consist in a rule of construction long honored by judges.

Coke himself said that common law is founded on experience, so that it changes over time—borrowing here and shifting emphasis there. Natural law principles, though, are by definition deontological; they are abstracted from a concrete context and do not change based on efficacy or "fit" with a given situation. If they did change, they would come ungrounded from natural law. By tying common law to natural law exclusively, we distort the meaning of both. Moreover, as McDowell points out, the natural law of John Locke and the natural law cited in the Declaration of Independence are products of a different time than the sources of custom and tradition revered by Coke. In Corwin's defense, we could say that he articulated a tension between the notion of a "living constitution" that is highly dependent on the judicial personalities of a particular time period on the one hand,

and the claim that higher principles hold the constitutional order together over time on the other. He did not resolve this tension, but he did explore it in his "higher law" article and his later work. Perhaps it asks too much of Corwin to reconcile these two tendencies within his notion of higher law constitutionalism. After all, the remainder of the twentieth century after Corwin wrote saw legal scholars striving to locate the precise balance between what they would call "attitudinal" and "doctrinal" influences on Supreme Court decision making. A justice who drew on tradition and learning in a wise and prudent manner might fit the bill drawn up by Corwin—and such a justice would also conform closely to Coke's description of the ideal practitioner of common law reason.

Conceptions of Natural Law

Because natural law features prominently in the thought of early modern legal theorists, it will be useful at this point to delineate some of the strands of natural law theory that we are familiar with today to see how they square with earlier usages. Natural law conceptions of rights require a ground, a metaphysical foundation that guarantees their truth. As I suggested earlier, one way to conceptualize this ground is to think of it in the form of an omnipotent being who reveals truths to humans. Certain laws are "natural," in this version, because a *divine power* has ordained them. The biblical teaching that humans are made in the image of God leads to precepts about how people should be treated, and those precepts are particularly clear examples of natural law proceeding from a grounding in a theological foundation.

Alternatively, natural law grounded in *reason* allows us to deduce truths about human nature that are objectively determinable and guaranteed to be correct by the laws of logic or the scientific method. What guarantees these truths is the objective and universal status of reason, which, like divine will, has often been seen as unquestionable.

Yet another alternative, which is often referred to as "modern natural law," derives its universal truth value from assumptions about the *essence of the human condition*. Humans *as humans* carry with them an entitlement to be treated with dignity and respect, to have their liberties honored, and this entitlement is inalienable. Interestingly, the Declaration of Independence invokes two of these conceptions when it says that "all men are by nature free and independent, endowed by their creator with certain inalienable rights." And John Locke grounded his conception of natural law in "both 'God and Reason,' which again provide a dual source of authoritativeness for Locke's principles."[15] Natural law is an appealing source of legal authority because it posits a ground, a universally applicable guarantee of the correctness of the position that one wishes to advance. And because the ground stands prior to human action, legislative acts cannot displace the entitlements that stem from it. It is at once both vague and compelling.[16]

Colonial Constitutionalism

As we examine the beliefs about rights and liberties circulating in the American colonies and the early Republic, it is tempting to superimpose a master narrative on the development of American constitutionalism—to speak, for example, of "the shift from the organic, unwritten British constitution to the defined and enumerated written American Constitution."[17] What actually happened, however, was more gradual. Developments in political thought occurring within the colonies influenced the development of American constitutionalism even before the American Constitution itself came into existence—which is to say that they had a conception of constitutionalism that looked back to the notion of "constitution" in English law. In the latter part of the seventeenth century, the American colonies came to refer more and more to each of their own governing documents as a "charter," whereas such a document previously was called a "patent." Both terms referred to political authority granted by the British Crown, but as the colonists came to prefer "charter," they also emphasized colonial governmental authority over its people.[18] Mary Sarah Bilder notes that this usage was consistent with, and reflective of, the then-current custom of spelling Magna Carta as "Magna Charta," "which reinforced this association between a charter and ancient liberties and authority."[19] Colonial charters were, like the Great Charter itself, a source of liberties of ancient provenance, reflected in a governing document. And this influence went beyond symbolic reverence; the Magna Carta was given binding force in legal proceedings. A. E. Dick Howard has shown that in seventeenth-century Virginia, the colonial governor reviewed legislation to be sure that it comported with "Magna Charta."[20] And in Massachusetts, the 1641 Body of Liberties followed the Magna Carta closely in its enumeration of liberties: not only due process but also the right to a speedy trial and some even more specific provisions concerning such matters as fines and fishing rights.[21] In Maryland, the Carolinas, New York, and New Jersey, "Magna Carta had by the end of the seventeenth century become embedded in the legal and constitutional ethos."[22] Colonial governors were charged with violating Magna Carta, and colonial statutes affirmed the Magna Carta's provisions protecting individual liberty. As colonists claimed for themselves the "rights of Englishmen," they took the Magna Carta's "law of the land" provision to be primary among the advantages of that inheritance. Thus, there is continuity between colonial and subsequent constitutionalism, even if the creation of the Republic with its written constitution was a significant change. The Magna Carta's influence on legal thought was one source of this continuity.

But what exactly was the ground for the Magna Carta's legal standing, and what made it binding? Did it reflect ancient liberties, as was often said? If these liberties had always existed, it would seem proper to consider them based in natural law. Did the Magna Carta therefore recognize natural right? The connection between natural law and natural right is problematic for some scholars studying seventeenth-century English/American legal history. For one thing, they note that legal discourse during that time did not articulate subjective rights as we think of them today. In 1670, as he was embroiled in legal controversy with the Crown, William Penn cited the Magna Carta in his own defense, but even though he was defending what we would now call the right of free assembly, he did not explain it that way.[23] Penn's writings "employed venerable terms like 'liberty' and 'privilege' as synonyms for this new concept [of subjective rights]. Where one would expect to find natural rights, Penn used 'natural privileges,' 'natural and civil common privileges,' 'paramount privileges,' or phrases such as the 'grand pillars of English liberty' and 'fundamental vital privileges.'"[24]

Penn's commentary on the Magna Carta, published in 1687, straddles the line between earlier thinking about freedom and liberty and the more precisely defined conception of rights that we would see in the Declaration of Independence and the U.S. Constitution. In the earlier rights language it was often possible to discern common law roots, so that rights were defined by tradition, and this included the Magna Carta's invocation of the common law.[25] This understanding of rights entailed "custom," "changeless time," "a view of the past in which civil rights existed in a timeless infinity, a frozen history without origins."[26] This description does not sound like the textually based conception of rights that developed in the American constitution and gained its more precise shape through Supreme Court jurisprudence. In other words, common law constitutionalism as we understand it today is not so vague or changeless. It does remain tied to the written text, even if judges look outside the text as they apply it. But the prerevolutionary common law rights language was different from the rights language that developed as the Bill of Rights was later applied and interpreted. The earlier version shared a similarity with the Lockean view of rights in that both conceptions held rights to be prepolitical and not of recent creation. However, there was an important difference. Locke taught that rights enabled *resistance* of tradition rather than binding obligation to it.[27] This resistance of tradition can be seen as one reason Locke became popular and influential among revolutionary statesman-thinkers.

It seems clear that the theories explaining how people came to have rights were as varied as the language used to describe the rights themselves. At times, American colonists claimed the "rights of Englishmen."[28] At other times, they appealed to rights held from "time immemorial"—a claim both hard to refute and hard to enforce. And we must keep in mind that rights language was deployed for different purposes. Sometimes the efforts were rhetorical, as colonial leaders sought to gain support for oppositional stances toward the British government. It would be a mistake to take all of those usages as explorations of political philosophy. Even when legal issues were at stake, as in the controversy over British "writs of assistance," there was an ideological component to the ways in which colonial leaders spoke of rights relative to the Crown.

Rights Language in 1776

By the time the Declaration of Independence was issued, some elements of rights language, and of American constitutionalism, had crystallized. Parliament's actions against the colonies provided a focal point for dissent but also drew a contrast between two views of "constitution." The Americans favored "the old English constitution of custom, prescription and contract," but that older form was being eclipsed by a new one: "a constitution of sovereign command and of arbitrary parliamentary supremacy."[29] Primus suggests that to some extent, the oppressive actions taken by Parliament against the American colonies actually helped to *generate* rights language, as the people translated their felt sense of injustice into rhetorically and legally efficacious language.[30] One other important change—and a readily understandable one—was the declining popularity of the practice of citing the "rights of Englishmen" as a basis for rights claims. As the colonies moved toward independence from Britain, they were less inclined to claim British legal lineage.[31] They sought to differentiate themselves rather than assimilate.

The Declaration of Independence itself contains a reference to constitutionalism that provides insight into the linkage between English and American constitutionalism. As the Declaration lists its arguments for independence, it alleges that the colonies were "subjected to a jurisdiction foreign to *our constitution*" (emphasis added). Stoner notes that earlier drafts of the document showed "our constitutions" (in the plural), and he takes this reference in both of its forms "to mean, as the term then meant when used in reference to the British, the whole amalgam of offices, principles, and fundamental laws that give the polity its form."[32] This reading seems most plausible, and it suggests an orientation of the common law mind shared by the Declaration's authors and the English commentators preceding them. Even if a direct line of influence cannot be traced from Coke to John Marshall as Edward Corwin would have it, it seems clear nonetheless that an understanding of common law constitutionalism in which tradition, precedent (including Magna Carta), and other unwritten law were all component parts crossed the Atlantic and took hold in the colonies.

Following the War of Independence and the constitutional period, two trends contributed to the development of American—as opposed to British—constitutionalism. These were the publication of court decisions and the use of judicial review. Bilder sums up the result of these developments as follows: "Out of the great binary pairs of English law—*lex scripta* and *lex non scripta*, common law and statutory law, slowly grew another far more powerful legal construct, Constitutional law, with unconstitutional its sole opposing companion."[33] Constitutional case law was an artifact of this new legal domain. And of course, we should not take Bilder's statement to mean that there had been no constitutional tradition prior to independence. Rather, the constitutional/unconstitutional binary pair formed a structural part of American courts as an institution as well as American constitutionalism.

The institutional changes I have mentioned amount to procedural components of American constitutionalism that stand alongside and complement the substantive aspects sketched out above. It goes without saying that the body of constitutional law developed through judicial review and compiled in a public case reporting system was essential for a tradition of judicial protection of individual rights. In particular, habeas corpus and due process protections survived and flourished in American constitutional law because of the institutional forms of judicial review and case reports. Eight hundred years after they were set forth in the Magna Carta, they are still relevant as a result of those institutional developments.

Howard sums up the changing role of Magna Carta in the early Republic as follows: "In the 18th century, the Charter was at the very core of colonial arguments and documents. It was invoked in the way lawyers would have used it, as precedent and authority. After Independence, its force was at one step removed."[34] See Table 2.1.

TABLE 2.1
CONTRASTING AMERICAN RIGHTS DISCOURSE: MID-1600S TO LATE 1700S

Mid-1600s	*Late 1700s*
Rights language: liberties, privileges	Rights language: subjective rights
Sources of rights: "Rights of Englishmen," colonial charters, Magna Carta, natural law	Sources of rights: U.S. Constitution, Magna Carta, natural law
Constitutionalism based on: custom, tradition, English precedent, natural law	Constitutionalism based on: U.S. Constitution, emerging precedent, natural law

Blackstone and the Rise of Liberalism

In the 1760s, another important analysis of the common law appeared in England. William Blackstone published his *Commentaries on the Law of England*, which proved even more directly influential than Coke's treatise for the founders of the American republic. With a century and a half of legal-philosophical thought (not to mention actual court decisions) separating him from Edward Coke, Blackstone (1723–1780)[35] was far better positioned to incorporate developments of emerging liberalism into his analysis. In fact, a major part of Blackstone's purpose was to address some of the tensions between the common law (with its emphasis on tradition, its unwritten rules, and its complex forms of pleading) and the positive law generated by Parliament. It is generally accepted that Blackstone held Parliament to be supreme when its actions conflicted with individual claims of right. In a well-known and oft-cited passage, Blackstone said that "if the parliament, will positively enact a thing to be done, which is unreasonable, I know of no power that can control it."[36] Thus did he differ from Coke in the way he ranked common law and statute: Parliament was supreme. While both thinkers acknowledged the important role of the common law in the English legal system, only Coke thought that it could trump an act of Parliament or an action of the Crown.

Duncan Kennedy argues that as Blackstone tried to reconcile the common law with emerging ideas about popular sovereignty, voluntary action, and legal positivism that were associated with liberalism, he actually functioned as an ideological agent of that nascent legal/social order. Kennedy reads the *Commentaries* as "an instrument of apology—an attempt to mystify both dominators and dominated by convincing them of the naturalness, the freedom and the rationality, of a condition of bondage."[37] On this view, Blackstone is what Gramsci called an "organic intellectual": a member of a social group who helps the group to become and remain dominant by explaining the world in a way that justifies that dominance.[38] Naturalizing inequality is one kind of explanation that could work in this way.

Kennedy makes it clear that his criticism of Blackstone is not aimed at refuting Blackstone's arguments in defense of the legal order. Instead, Kennedy wants to show the ideological work that the *Commentaries* do. "It is to discover not what should have been done, but first the apologetic motive that the formal rationale was designed to disguise, and second the contribution of the reasoning process to the creation and maintenance of the liberal mode of mediation."[39] The "mediation" Kennedy refers to here arises out of what he calls the "fundamental contradiction" of social existence. Individuals find fulfillment and support in living among others, but the collective surrounding individuals is also a threat to their individuality. This is the inescapable contradiction of the human condition. The contradiction is ever-present in human experience, but it is mediated in modernity by rights theory.[40] A scheme of enforceable individual rights allows us to live with, and benefit from, a community offering social support while also keeping others at arm's length and guaranteeing that we will not be swallowed up by the collective. Kennedy is of course skeptical of this claim of mediation, but he is less interested in refuting the claim on its merits and more interested in showing how it functions to maintain a set of power relations.

Morton Horwitz has observed that judges as well as (and perhaps even more than) commentators performed an ideological role in shaping early American law. Judicial opinions explained and justified developments in the common law that "direct[ed] the course of social change." And, of course, these rulings were not scholarly treatises but rather judicial orders that carried the force of law—both for the case at bar and as precedent for the future. In the early Republic, "common law decision making had taken on many of the qualities of legislation."[41] Horwitz sees this lawmaking activity facilitating the growth of an industrial economy, with judges as agents of this transformation. He emphasizes private law of torts and contracts rather than constitutional law, which he thinks has already been thoroughly studied.[42] But of course the overlap of constitutional questions with private commercial activity is extensive, as we see in such areas as economic substantive due process. Kennedy and Horwitz ask us to consider two questions that arise at two levels of analysis. First, what interests are served by certain legal rulings in economically related cases? Second, how did the ideological work of judges and commentators help to explain rules and outcomes in ways that made those rules and outcomes acceptable to society?

The strongest version of this thesis is that law is instrumental to domination, and domination is supported by "apologetic moves" that justify existing power relations. There can be no real question that law is potentially instrumental to domination. The barest form of law—sovereign's command—has long accomplished domination of the subjects of the realm. But as a force that potentially binds all actors, law is not predetermined toward domination. The Magna Carta itself came into being as a counterforce to unlimited sovereign prerogative. Thus, while law contains within it a tendency toward domination, that tendency can be resisted. The terrain on which legal constructs are articulated is open and contested.

I have included what I would call ideologically attuned critiques of English and American legal development here because they are powerful and persuasive, and because they provide a shift in perspective that allows the observer to see the ways that law works within the larger society beyond the courtroom, beyond the lives of the parties involved in a particular legal dispute. This larger perspective is really what constitutionalism is most vitally about, for we are interested not merely in predicting how the Supreme Court might decide some future case but in how institutional development proceeds and how that development bears on the lives of citizens. If commentators and judges engage in "apologetic moves," it is worthwhile to determine what those moves conceal. If their explanations impact others, we need to assess those impacts.

The critical perspective does raise some questions that are very difficult to answer. First, if Blackstone and Supreme Court justices are acting ideologically, on whose behalf are they acting? Do they merely reflect class position in their outlook and preference (as in the attitudinal view of judicial behavior), or are they self-consciously promoting certain interests above others? To ask these questions is to embark on a course that deviates from this study of common law constitutionalism and explores the (problematic) claims of ideology critique. Without committing to that detour, it is nonetheless possible to comment briefly on constitutionalism and idcology. If we take the study of ideology to be the study of the relationships between ideas and power, then it becomes important to understand the effects of certain statements on belief systems. What judges and authoritative commentators say about law will be important in this regard. Someone studying ideology could conclude that all constitutional meaning is determined by the pronouncements of judges and commentators, and also that all of this meaning construction is calculated to serve the interests of powerful groups in society. Few people would make the claim of ideological influence this strongly, but less totalizing versions can be found. The most problematic part of this argument is not that powerful groups fare better in the legal system, or that commentators apologize for this inequality, but that *apologetic statements facilitate inequality*. In this regard it matters whether the commentator is a judge or not, because judges are in a position to pronounce legal outcomes that carry the force of law whether they are persuasive or not, whereas commentators can only urge the adoption of their own point of view. And once a ruling has been made, it has the force of inertia behind it. Two questions arise here: First, how much space is there for legal meanings to develop that do not support the interests of the powerful? Second, to what extent does ideological work shape or constrain that space? We need not provide a full answer to those questions in order to assert that institutional norms like constitutionalism have a force of their own that cannot be fully controlled by ideology. Rights claims remain valuable and efficacious to constitutional litigants even if rights are not evenly distributed across social groups in society. Doctrine still exerts a force on the mind of the judicial decision maker.[43] In short, we can acknowledge that ideological pronouncements can affect the development of legal rules without folding up the tent and going home—that is, abandoning the project of tracing the path of common law constitutionalism.

Conclusion

At this point in the study, it should be clear that English constitutionalism, with its wellspring in the Magna Carta, encouraged American thinkers and jurists in the colonial period to give weight to custom and tradition in their thinking about liberties. This earlier version of constitutionalism held that written documents such as the Magna Carta reflected and shaped the tradition of constitutionalism but did not by themselves fully define that tradition. In other words it is not simply that custom and tradition influence constitutional interpretation, but more than that: the constitution itself, on this earlier view, was not simply a written document. In fact, "constitution" was often opposed to positive law, as I have shown.

It should also be clear that the Americans emphasized *experience* as they sought to create and refine legal practices in the new Republic. The appeals to experience were frequent and diverse. James Wilson explicitly invoked experience as an important guide,[44] as did John Dickinson. "Accidents" and "experience" "were part of the ongoing historical process of constitutionalism," according to David Thomas Konig.[45] This emphasis will be evident in other periods in American constitutional development that I will examine in subsequent chapters, and it is important to my overall argument: that the strongest case for adhering to common law constitutionalism is a historical-pragmatic one. This case is made strongly by the early statesmen-thinkers, and it echoes through the other periods as well.

One other point bears mentioning here in summary. An additional insight that emerges from this consideration of written and unwritten law and their interplay is that constitutionalism as envisioned by the thinkers considered in this chapter has a dual orientation: it *protects* rights of individuals, but it also *restrains* individuals from doing what they might otherwise do in the state of nature. We are inclined to think first and foremost of the ways in which a constitutional tradition and a written constitution themselves safeguard civil and political rights, as the Bill of Rights promises to do. But the creation of a written constitution, as a specific point of departure from the absolute freedom enjoyed in the state of nature, is also a *limitation* on that freedom. As Rogers Smith puts it, constitutionalism denies "that all social purposes must forever be subordinated to individual freedom, with government confined to an umpire role aimed solely at maximizing freedom for all."[46] The Constitution protects freedoms, but it also enables the pursuit of public ends, such as the waging of war, representative democracy, taxation, and treaty making. Each of these ends is plainly a restraint on individual freedom in some sense, but each of them is also specifically sanctioned by the American Constitution. This dual use of state force in the constitutional tradition—restraining and liberating—comes into focus most clearly when we view it through the lens of early liberal depictions of the absolute freedom of the state of nature. Paradoxically, constitutionalism limits natural rights as well as protecting them.

3

The Slavery Question

> The existence of slavery under any shape is so repugnant to the natural rights of man and the dictates of justice, that it seems difficult to find for it any adequate justification.
>
> Justice Story, *Miscellaneous Writings of Joseph Story*

> This dominion is essential to the value of slaves as property, to the security of the master, and to the public tranquility, greatly dependent upon their subordination; and in fine, as most effectually securing the general protection and comfort of the slaves themselves.
>
> Judge Ruffin in *State v. Mann*

There are several reasons why nineteenth-century debates over slavery, and the eventual resolution of those debates by the Civil War, form a crucial chapter in the story of common law constitutionalism and the Magna Carta legacy. First, of course, is the fundamental problem of a constitution that proclaims enforceable individual rights while also acknowledging and permitting slavery. Second are the numerous references to natural law (often contrasted with positive law) in the context of the moral and legal status of slavery. As discussed in chapter 2, natural law theories assume that law proceeds from an ultimate source or ground that cannot be challenged: God, truth, reason, or nature.

In this view, law is unchanging. Positive law theories, by contrast, hold that law proceeds from an authorized lawmaking act, such as a legislative body voting to enact it. Third, judicial opinions produced during the period, such as *The Antelope*, *State v. Mann*, *Commonwealth v. Aves*, *Prigg v. Pennsylvania*, and *Dred Scott v. Sandford*, proved highly significant in the development of constitutional tradition. Finally, prominent voices in the debates, such as Justices Story and Curtis, specifically discussed the Magna Carta and its key legacies of habeas corpus, due process, and the right to a jury trial. Thus, the antebellum period forms an important juncture in Magna Carta's influence on constitutional law in the United States.

Slavery and Natural Law

As a philosophical matter, the existence of slavery in a society professing to adhere to the rule of law, and to value individual rights, poses a quandary. This quandary produced ambivalence on the part of commentators writing during the constitutional period and the early years of the Republic. There was a need to explain how the institution of slavery could exist within the American experiment in liberal democracy without discrediting that experiment entirely. Some of the aspects of the legal discourse reflect attempts to reconcile the contradiction. Justice Story proclaimed that slavery was contrary to natural right, as Lord Mansfield had also said in *Sommersett's Case*, and even state court judges in the slave states agreed.[1] Counterposed to the natural law prohibition of slavery was its authorization by positive law (which is often referred to in this contcxt as "municipal law"). In other words, judges found themselves bound to uphold laws that were contrary to their sense of justice and contrary to natural law because those laws had been enacted by a legislative majority. There is nothing unusual in this judicial response, since the judicial role in a system of separated and balanced powers is to discern and apply the legislative will. However, we have already seen in Coke's discussion of the common law that he would consider the effect of common law rules on the meaning of positive law. In *Bonham's Case*, Coke interpreted the positive law (a royal grant of power to the London College of Physicians) in light of common law principles of justice; it was those principles that gave shape to his reading of the written law. In that case, it was possible to read the law in such a way as not to invalidate it entirely. The two rules—common law and written law—could be reconciled so that both remained standing. There are other instances where the conflict is more direct. For example, a state law protecting the right to own slaves would conflict directly with the natural right to bodily liberty, and a judge ruling in favor of natural right would have to deny effect to the statute. Later, this would be a rather straightforward application of judicial review: finding a conflict between the constitution and a statute, and declaring the statute unconstitutional. But in the years leading up to the Civil War, judicial review was not routinely understood in this way, at least with regard to the Bill of Rights (although the majority in *Dred Scott v. Sandford* invalidated the Missouri Compromise through judicial review). In any event, when faced with this conflict of law, judges protested that municipal law must displace natural law rather than the other way around.

The Naturalization of Slavery in State v. Mann

Another alternative to acknowledging that slavery violates natural law would be to naturalize slavery as a hybrid of natural and municipal (positive) law, as did the court in the North Carolina case of *State v. Mann*. This case arose as a criminal action for battery against a slave owner who had beaten a slave. In overturning the conviction, Judge Ruffin confessed to feeling a "struggle" between "the feelings of the man, and the duty of the magistrate."[2] This confession echoes the pronouncements by other courts that slavery violates natural law. Like those other statements, Ruffin's "feelings of the man" seem to proceed from a deeply felt sense of justice that recoils against actions treating slaves as less than human. Here, the issue was that the slave, named Lydia, had been beaten "excessively."[3]

And yet the court found itself powerless to intervene and compelled to release the defendant from guilt. In part this was based on the existence of positive law, "until it shall seem fit to the Legislature to interpose express enactments to the contrary."[4] But this particular recourse to positive law reverses the presumption stated by other courts and cited earlier: that slavery violates natural law and can only exist where *created* by positive law. *State v. Mann*, by contrast, places the burden on the state to enact positive law that will *change* the status quo by *prohibiting* slavery. "Until then, it will be the imperative duty of the Judges to recognize the full dominion of the master over the slave." Ruffin continues: "This dominion is essential to the value of slaves as property, to the security of the master, and to the public tranquility, greatly dependent upon their subordination; and in fine, as most effectually securing the general protection and comfort of the slaves themselves."[5] How else can this passage be read other than as a naturalization of the master-slave relationship? Ruffin is not describing a condition induced by legislative act but rather an "order of things" that could only be displaced by an explicit act of government. The power of the master "is in no instance, usurped; but is conferred by the laws of man at least, if not by the law of God."[6] I have called this conception a hybrid of a naturalized understanding of slavery and a positive law–based justification for it because the opinion in *State v. Mann* is not entirely clear which view predominates. On the same page, the court suggests that the legislature could end the practice of

felt he could not effectively address the Opinion of the Court, since he did not have the published version available to him as he wrote his dissent.[12] Notwithstanding this disadvantage, Curtis's dissent was widely considered an effective rebuttal of the majority opinion, and as the *Dred Scott* case became increasingly discredited with the passage of time, Curtis's opinion seemed even more prescient.

A decade after his resignation from the bench, Curtis was enlisted to defend President Andrew Johnson in Johnson's Senate trial on impeachment charges. Curtis did so successfully and thereby delivered a rebuke to the congressional majority who wanted Johnson to pursue Reconstruction more vigorously. Thus it is difficult to characterize Benjamin Curtis as consistently siding with pro-slavery or antislavery factions in the Civil War years. Moreover, Streichler provides evidence, gleaned from private correspondence, that Curtis's views toward African Americans were uncharitable at best and would more accurately be called racist.[13] Any appraisal of Curtis's views, works, and leanings would have to conclude that "he displayed little sensitivity to the human face of the tragedy" of American slavery and its aftermath.[14] But we are more interested, here, in Curtis's role in the development of American constitutionalism. In this regard, his dissent in *Dred Scott* "foreshadowed the great transformation of the Constitution from a charter that protected slavery to one which guaranteed racial equality."[15] As we will see, this transformation relied on common law constitutionalism and drew support from the Magna Carta tradition in particular. First, though, it is necessary to review some of the slavery-related court decisions preceding *Dred Scott*.

Sommersett's Case *(1772)*

Although this case was heard and decided in England, its importance for American legal development was apparent immediately.

The case involved a slave, James Sommersett, who had come to England with his master (Stewart) from Jamaica, where slavery was practiced. As they made ready to depart from England, Sommersett escaped Stewart's custody in order to remain in England. He was captured and placed aboard a slave ship bound for Jamaica, where he was to be sold as a slave.[16] Sommersett filed a habeas corpus action seeking his freedom, he was brought from the custody of the slave ship's captain to the court, and the case was heard before Lord Mansfield.[17] According to Judge Higginbotham, "The precise issue was whether it was legal for a slave master from another country to forcibly remove his slave from England."[18] Counsel for Sommersett, Francis Hargrave, cited the decline of villeinage (a condition resembling slavery in many respects) in Europe as evidence of the disapprobation with which servitude of various forms was viewed by the late eighteenth century, and of "the preference of the common law for freedom."[19]

After citing authority to the contrary in the form of a 1729 advisory opinion (which he gives "due respect"), Mansfield says, in reference to the practice of slavery, "It is so odious, that nothing can be suffered to support it, but positive law." Then he concludes, "Whatever inconveniences, therefore, may follow from the decision, I cannot say this case is allowed or approved by the law of England; and therefore the black must be discharged."[20] There are two significant developments here. First, Mansfield states what American courts will later say repeatedly: that slavery can only be supported by positive law. This ruling helps to solidify the common law principle that slavery is against natural law. Second, and perhaps greater in practical impact, Mansfield finds that Sommersett's presence on free soil renders him free of the chains of slavery, even though he had not been freed by his master, Stewart, or otherwise emancipated previously. Although it is difficult to glean this import from the tersely worded decision in *Sommersett*, it does furnish precedent for the proposition, which was cited by the dissenters in *Dred Scott*, that residence in a free state rendered a slave free as a matter of common law.

Higginbotham notes that the precise holding in *Sommersett* was narrow: it "merely prohibit[ed] a master's attempt to kidnap or imprison his slave when seeking to remove the slave from England."[21] Would the decision disturb or threaten the foreign slave trade or the social relations of slavery in the colonies or in other parts of the world? Subsequent decisions showed that though English courts were often willing to hold *Sommersett* to mean that slavery ends when a slave enters England,[22] they were not generally inclined to extend the ruling in *Sommersett* to a broader condemnation of the slave trade. In particular, Higginbotham notes that the *Slave Grace* case, decided in 1827, held that a slave from Antigua who came to England but who returned "voluntarily" to Antigua would resume her slave status upon her return.[23] Of course, Higginbotham notes, the matter of "voluntary leaving" is somewhat problematic, since this would seem to mean that anyone not forcibly removed was leaving voluntarily, when in fact they were not truly leaving of their own free will but rather at the direction of the slave master.[24] In any case, events in England were moving toward total prohibition of slavery, as the Foreign Slave Trade Bill of 1807 declared the slave trade to be "contrary to the principles of justice, humanity and sound policy." By an 1833 law, slavery was abolished throughout the British colonies (which no longer included the American colonies, obviously).[25] The English experience, then, provided precedent for antislavery interpretation of the common law as well as antislavery modification to positive law. What was the effect of these precedents in the United States?

The Antelope *(1825)*

This was another case where, like *State v. Mann*, the Court admitted to feeling a conflict between the demands of the law and a deeper sense of justice. After an American vessel seized a cargo of slaves from various foreign ships, it fell to the Court to determine the fate of those slaves. Should they be returned to claimants from Spain and Portugal, or should they be released and made subject to the laws of the United States?[26] Chief Justice Marshall declined to declare the slave trade contrary to the law of nations and instead ordered some of the slaves returned to Spain. He did say that slavery was contrary to natural law, but he also pointed out that the trade in slaves was tolerated by the law and therefore slave traders had a right to expect their property to be recognized and protected by the law. The import of this decision is that Marshall took the law of nations to include positive law and customary trade practices as well as the common law and natural law principles enunciated in *Sommersett*. Thus, the Court had an opportunity to make an antislavery statement and precedent, but it declined to do so. Complicating the matter was the fact that foreign nations were involved, and therefore the ruling would have diplomatic repercussions as well. In any event, the significance for the purposes of this study is that Marshall recognized the pull of natural law but declined to yield to it.

Commonwealth v. Aves *(1836)*

Courts in the Northern states generally followed *Sommersett's* lead and ruled "sojourners' slaves and fugitives" would become free upon entering a free state.[27] Justice McLean, dissenting in the *Dred Scott* case, lists a line of authorities ruling to that effect.[28] The case of *Commonwealth v. Aves* tested this proposition in 1836, when abolitionists in Boston filed suit seeking the freedom of a six-year-old child slave from Louisiana who was visiting Boston with her master.[29] Lemuel Shaw ruled in favor of the child, basing his ruling on the natural law repugnance toward slavery, the prohibition against slavery in the Massachusetts

Constitution, and the length of time the child stayed in Massachusetts. Justice Curtis argued the opposing side, dwelling in his argument on the tolerance for slavery reflected in the Fugitive Slave Clause of the Constitution. In the end, this case followed *Sommersett* and lent its name to the line of precedent holding that residence in a free state made one free.

Prigg v. Pennsylvania *(1842)*

In this case, a slave catcher challenged Pennsylvania's 1826 antikidnapping law, under which he had been prosecuted for forcibly capturing a runaway slave and her children. The law specified procedures by which Pennsylvania state courts would determine the status of an alleged fugitive rather than leaving the resolution of these matters to forcible self-help measures. The plaintiff in error (slave catcher Edward Prigg) made three alternative arguments:

- The Fugitive Slave Clause of the Constitution (Article IV, Section 2) gave Congress complete authority in the field and precluded any state law touching the subject.
- The Fugitive Slave Law of 1793, which was passed in enforcement of the constitutional provision, precluded any state law touching the subject.
- Even if concurrent legislative authority existed in the states and federal government in this field, the Pennsylvania law conflicted with federal law and was therefore superseded.[30]

Justice Story wrote a majority opinion favoring Prigg. He began by citing the positive law basis of slavery: "The state of slavery is deemed to be a mere municipal regulation, founded upon and limited to the range of the territorial laws. This was fully recognized in *Somerset's Case*."[31] The *Prigg* case, then, is one of the American constitutional law decisions that adopted *Sommersett's* premise regarding the legal basis of slavery: that it was contrary to natural law and only supported by positive law. As a result, not only the substance of that premise but also English common law constructions of natural law found their way into Supreme Court jurisprudence—common law constitutionalism helped to generate an American version.

Despite this linkage to liberty in English common law, the outcome in *Prigg* was not so fortunate for the antislavery side. On the merits of the case, Story interpreted the constitutional text to "manifestly contemplate[ ] the existence of a positive, unqualified right on the part of the owner of the slave which no state law or regulation can in any way qualify, regulate, control, or restrain."[32] Here, Story prioritizes the property right of the slave master over any other rights that may be implicated in fugitive slave disputes (e.g., procedural, trial-related rights of the fugitive). Story seems to naturalize the master-slave relationship, as Judge Ruffin did earlier, by according such controlling significance to the slave master's property rights. Story assumes that the Constitution *must* be read to rank order the relevant rights claims in this way. It seems that the right of the slave master assumes priority in Story's mind based on a philosophical ground that is not fully articulated in his opinion for the Court. Story's own antislavery views notwithstanding, he elevated the racialized social order of his time and place to become the natural order of things, so that he could assume, without explaining why, that the slave master's right is absolute.

Story connects the alternative grounds of the plaintiff's case to make the case impenetrable. He says that even though the constitutional grant of power to protect the master's property rights "require[s] no aid from legislation," enforcement is contemplated by Article IV and must come from the federal government.[33] In several places in the opinion, Story affirms that power over fugitive slave enforcement is granted to the federal government exclusively.[34] Thus, the terms of the Fugitive Slave Law of 1793, which was passed in enforcement of Article IV, provides a separate, statutory basis for denying the state legislature of Pennsylvania the power to regulate in this area. Finally, the majority opinion warns that state enforcement would lead to uneven results in which differences in state procedures would further endanger the ability of slave masters to recover fugitive slaves in the free states. Although the "owner has the same security, and the same remedial justice, and the same exemption from state regulation" in every state, each time he crosses a state boundary, "he becomes amenable to the laws of another sovereignty whose regulations may greatly embarrass or delay the exercise of his rights."[35] This potential inconsistency in enforcement provides a policy-based reason for Story to say that the Pennsylvania law and similar laws in other states are an undesirable alternative to exclusively federal regulation.

William Wiecek notes that the Pennsylvania antikidnapping law was motivated at least in part by Maryland and Pennsylvania officials' desire for an agreeable system for extraditing fugitive slaves—and Story adverts to this fact in the opinion itself. But abolitionists in Pennsylvania saw an opportunity to strengthen protections for slaves and others in these disputes, and so they sought input into the legislative process. The result was a law that nominally pursued interests of both sides but was seen as too burdensome by slave masters.[36]

Justice McLean dissented from the majority opinion. As Justin Dyer points out, McLean focused on the harm that the Pennsylvania statute sought to address: the violence resulting from forcible capture of suspected fugitives, as well as the kidnapping of free blacks who would then be carried off and enslaved.[37] These free persons, who were also potential victims of fugitive slave enforcement, would suffer rights violations that connected directly to Article 39/40 of the Magna Carta: unavailability of habeas corpus and deprivation of the right to jury trial. In fact, the kidnapping of free blacks in Pennsylvania had already been documented. The Pennsylvania law would have protected their rights to some extent by instituting legal process before an alleged fugitive slave could be removed from within Pennsylvania's borders. By invalidating the Pennsylvania statute, the Court had opened up the possibility that free persons in that state would be deprived of liberty "without a jury trial" and contrary to "the law of the land." Thus, McLean sought to preserve the linkage in American constitutionalism between constitutionally protected liberties and common law foundations of freedom in the Magna Carta.[38]

Dyer explains that Justice Story himself, as well as Story's son, saw the *Prigg* opinion differently—as a *pro*-liberty decision. This is because it federalized the fugitive slave issue and also distinguished between fugitive slaves and slaves traveling with a slave master, so that only the former but not the latter were covered by the constitutional provision (Article IV) protecting a slave master's property rights.[39] In any event, the majority opinion in *Prigg* has a dual significance for common law constitutionalism. It incorporates what Higginbotham called "the preference of the common law for freedom" while also strengthening the rights of slave masters at the expense of slaves and others.[40]

Meanwhile, states dealt differently with issues of capture, extradition, and return of suspected fugitive slaves. In 1823, a federal court in South Carolina struck down an extreme measure said to have been inspired by fears of slave rebellion. Under that state law, the Negro Seaman's Act of 1822, officials at the Port of Charleston were required to seize any free black seaman who landed there and imprison him until the ship cleared. The shipmaster would be required to pay him out of confinement or he would be sold into slavery. This law was found to violate the federal commerce power as well as treaty obligations.[41]

Dred Scott v. Sandford *(1857)*

In terms of the overall struggle against slavery, the issuance of the *Dred Scott* decision was both a setback and a polarizing event. Chief Justice Taney wrote an opinion for the majority (though each justice also wrote separately) that was wholly favorable to Sandford, the slave master. He denied that Scott was (or could be) a citizen of the United States and therefore ruled that Scott could not sue for his freedom. Then Taney went further and declared the Missouri Compromise unconstitutional. The decision was polarizing because of its stark terms. Taney emphasized again and again his view that black Americans had no legal status other than as property. He believed that they were not citizens, could not be citizens, had played no part in the formation of the Republic, could claim no rights whatsoever, and held an inherently inferior status to whites that could never be altered. This emphatically and contemptuously stated position reinforced battle lines between pro-slavery and antislavery forces and focused the opposition on Taney's intransigent views. Moreover, the ruling on the Missouri Compromise was seen as dicta—statements extraneous to the holding in the case and therefore unnecessary. Because Taney's ruling on Scott's citizenship disposed of the matter in controversy, it seemed that he had gone out of his way, even after the dispute between Scott and Sandford had been resolved, to aid the pro-slavery side by prohibiting Congress from legislating on the status of slavery. This overreaching had been evident, too, in the *Prigg* case discussed earlier, where Taney concurred in the judgment striking down the Pennsylvania antikidnapping law but wrote separately to emphasize that southern states should still be free to regulate slave seizure and extradition by state law. His vote in that case was to disallow a law *protecting* blacks against unlawful seizure but to allow laws that made their seizure and removal easier. He took positions that were inconsistent doctrinally in terms of federalism but consistent in favoring the rights of slave-owning white Americans over black Americans both enslaved and free.

The facts of the *Dred Scott* case are familiar. Scott was enslaved in the slave state of Missouri, and he traveled to Illinois (a free state) with Emerson, his master. He also lived in the Wisconsin territory, married (with Emerson's approval), and had children by the marriage. Scott returned eventually to Missouri with Emerson. After Emerson's death, Scott sued for his freedom, claiming that his residence on free soil had emancipated him from slavery. The defendant Sandford, who by the time the litigation commenced held title to Scott as property, countered Scott's complaint by saying that Scott was not a citizen of Missouri and therefore could not sue in its courts. When the Missouri Supreme Court sided with Sandford, Scott requested that the U.S. Supreme Court review that decision. Chief Justice Taney phrased the question as one of the right to bring suit. He asked whether "those persons who are the descendants of Africans who were imported into this country, and sold as slaves" were entitled to bring suit in the first place. To answer this question, Taney had to determine, first, whether they were citizens. His answer was emphatically negative:

> They are not included, and were not intended to be included, under the word "citizens" in the Constitution, and can therefore claim none of the rights and privileges which that instrument provides for and secures to citizens of the United States. On the contrary, they were at that time considered as a subordinate and inferior class of beings, who had been subjugated by the dominant race, and, whether emancipated or not, yet remained subject to their authority, and had no rights or privileges but such as those who held the power and the Government might choose to grant them.[42]

This passage is indicative of Taney's general tone in the opinion. Throughout the opinion, and particularly when discussing the legal status of black Americans, he seems to take every opportunity to emphasize what he sees as their lack of personhood by using terms such as "unfortunate," "unfit," "subordinate," "inferior," and "ordinary object of merchandise." And in contrast to the widespread views of others about slavery and natural law cited earlier in this chapter, Taney could say that his view of black Americans as undeserving of any rights was "regarded as an axiom in morals as well as in politics, which no one thought of disputing, or supposed to be open to dispute."[43] This rhetorical device of assuming, without showing it, universal agreement with his premises appears a number of times in the opinion: Taney says "no one supposed" or "no one would question" the contrary of what he asserts.[44]

As for the logic of Taney's opinion, it appears strained and gap-ridden to the twentieth-century reader. It is difficult to know how it might have sounded to readers in 1857 because we bring to it so much more historical perspective. However, there are a number of rather striking lapses, all of which are pointed out by the dissent:

- Taney does not acknowledge the force of the natural law argument against slavery.
- He does not explain adequately why the Missouri Supreme Court departed from precedent to rule that after residence in a free state, Scott remained a slave.
- His reading of Congress's power to legislate in the territories is most unpersuasive.
- His reading of American constitutional history is unsupported by evidence.

Some recent scholarship has revisited Taney's *Dred Scott* opinion and suggested that it was more centrist or pragmatic than conventional wisdom in the past has suggested.[45] This criticism emphasizes the chief justice's institutional role at a crisis point in American political development. In this context—that is, my assessment of common law constitutionalism—those critiques are somewhat beside the point as we trace assumptions and arguments about constitutional interpretation through U.S. history to show which ones have helped to advance and apply common law notions of freedom traceable to the Magna Carta via judicial review.

Thus, we turn to Justice Curtis's dissenting opinion in *Dred Scott*, which was influential in the short and long term. He proceeds methodically to address and rebut each of the arguments supporting the majority opinion. Curtis cites widely from English and American precedent, Coke and Blackstone, and the authority of natural right. He cites the *Sommersett* case in particular, for the proposition that slavery can only be authorized by positive law. And here, he uses common law constitutionalism in a novel way: to characterize slave owners' property rights as deserving of less protection than other rights. Due process, he says, refers to the expectation that ancient rights will be respected as against government intrusion. But if slavery (and its attendant property rights in slaves) can only be supported by positive law, then they are not among the property rights that the common law meaning of "due process" contemplates to protect.[46] Curtis says that due process

> is not peculiar to the Constitution of the United States; it was borrowed from Magna Charta; was brought to America by our ancestors, as part of their inherited liberties, and has existed in all the States, usually in the very words of the great charter. It existed in every political community in America in 1787, when the ordinance prohibiting slavery north and west of the Ohio was passed.[47]

So widespread state regulation had long limited the property rights of slave owners. Yet none of those laws "though they exist in many States, were ever supposed to be in conflict with the principle of Magna Charta incorporated into the State Constitutions."[48] Nor was the clause in Article I, Section 9 regulating the importation of slaves in 1808 ever challenged as violative of due process and therefore of Magna Carta. From the unchallenged existence of all of these modes of slavery regulation, Curtis concludes that the ancient lineage of due process does not encompass slave property. This acquiescence, alongside the positive law foundation of slavery, differentiates slave property from other kinds of property rights. By unlinking slave owners' rights from "due process," Curtis strips away from them a crucial layer of protection.

Probably the most important contribution Curtis made in his *Dred Scott* dissent was to provide proof that black Americans did, in fact, participate in ratification of the Constitution by voting to ratify. He did this by reviewing the historical record and showing that free blacks in at least some of the states were entitled to vote by the laws of the state, and that they were therefore part of the ratification process of the Constitution. This demonstration effectively rebutted Taney's assertion that black Americans "were not intended to be included, under the word 'citizens' in the Constitution."[49] Though the dissenting opinion was not legally binding, it was taken as authoritative by many people of the time, including future president Lincoln.[50]

McLean joined Curtis in dissent but wrote separately to emphasize certain differences in their positions. One of McLean's contributions was to attack directly the claims of special protections for property rights in slaves. As we have seen, these particular property rights were often asserted by Southerners to be of a special character—deserving of extra protection, or even inviolate. Kentucky's 1850 Constitution explicitly stated as much.

But McLean drew the natural/positive law argument out to its conclusion, suggesting that positive law could prohibit slavery just as it could authorize it. This argument echoes and reinforces Curtis's efforts to place slave owners' property rights in a different—and less secure—foundation than other constitutional rights that were given shape by the common law tradition.

McLean contributed to antislavery jurisprudence in *Prigg* and *Dred Scott*, but Curtis's *Dred Scott* opinion is better remembered, perhaps because it is more far-reaching. Streichler sums up the import of Curtis's dissent nicely, and his summary is worth quoting:

> The key to reading Curtis is to understand his opinion as an expression of possibilities rather than an exact solution: the federal judiciary had a potentially expansive role in enforcing the civil rights of black Americans, Congress had plenary power to exclude slavery from the territories, slavery was not protected as a property right under the Constitution, and blacks were "in every sense" among the people of the United States.[51]

Conclusion

The nineteenth-century Supreme Court decisions concerning slavery made a crucial early link between the Magna Carta and individual rights protections in American constitutionalism. This remains true despite the fact that individual litigants did not see their claims to freedom vindicated. Even while proclaiming themselves bound to uphold the property rights of slaveholders, Supreme Court justices and lower court judges repeatedly acknowledged that slavery violated natural law and could only be supported by positive law. Thus, where positive law did not exist, the common law with its "preference" for freedom would operate as a default rule against the existence of slavery. This is not to say that pro-slavery positive law would be easy to vanquish, or that jurists always kept these philosophical dividing lines clear. Rather, it is simply to suggest that a pro–individual liberty tradition originating in English common law (and memorialized in the Magna Carta) gained traction in U.S. constitutional law in the years leading up to the Civil War. This occurred through formulations advanced by Justices Curtis and McLean but also by decisional law that was formally pro-slavery, such as Justice Story's opinion in *Prigg v. Pennsylvania*. The discursive terrain on which slavery debates were fought remained open and contested—as, indeed, discourse supporting social relations always is. Participants such as Chief Justice Taney did their part to articulate rationales for supporting the slavery-based social order. They not only denied freedom to individual litigants like Dred Scott in the most dehumanizing terms but also put the force of the law behind the interests of the pro-slavery faction of American society. Thus, Taney and other jurists deployed state power in a particular direction while also working to make those deployments acceptable and legitimate.

However, when the idea of inherent human liberty was introduced into legal and political discourse in the American colonies and then the Republic, it was given further shape by the practices it helped to organize, such as the abolitionist movement. Slaveholders and pro-slavery segments of society sought to describe the practice of slavery and the legal status of slaves in ways that explained and justified the institution of slavery, but those meanings circulated in discourse alongside—and in conflict with—another set of meanings that emphasized what we would now call universal human rights. The activities of abolitionists in England and the United States emphasized the moral repugnance of slavery. Early on, Granville Sharp argued powerfully in print that slavery violated the English tradition of liberty. He cited "statutes ranging from the mid-14th century down to the Habeas Corpus Act (1679)" to argue that "all persons in England, including black slaves, had a statutory right to contest their restraints in the courts through the writ of habeas corpus. He thus constituted a link in a chain of descent from Magna Charta through the mediaeval Parliaments to the nineteenth century American antislavery movement and the origins of the due process and equal protection guarantees of the Fourteenth Amendment."[52]

The American antislavery movement in its various phases, too, helped to shape legal discourses about slavery. Wiecek notes that antislavery constitutionalism in the United States developed two branches. One was a moderate branch, which sought to oppose the extension of slavery but generally did not challenge the slaveholders' ability to practice slavery within the slave states. The radical constitutionalists, by contrast, developed a constitutional understanding that saw slavery as entirely antithetical to the U.S. Constitution. They had to address the references to slavery within the Constitution, of course, and they did so by arguing that the Constitution *in its essence* disfavored slavery—and this essence could be discerned by tracing the principles of the Declaration of Independence through to their embodiment in the Constitution.[53] In support of this argument, they drew on natural law formulations and on Blackstone, thus evoking the spirit of the English Constitution with its reliance on unwritten sources.[54] The radical abolitionists "failed" in the sense that they did not by themselves bring about an end to slavery (it took a war to do that); and it is true that their political influence as an organized group waned after 1848, but they "transmuted natural law concepts into working guarantees of individual freedom" that would later take shape in due process and equal protection jurisprudence.[55]

Their arguments impacted the views of judges, as we know from the statements of the judges themselves reflecting their uneasiness with the institution of slavery. But even as the judges were affected by social forces criticizing slavery and urging abolition, so too were abolitionists responsive to doctrinal developments in the case law. The relationship was recursive. We have seen, for example, the way the antislavery press received Justice Curtis's dissent in *Dred Scott.* Supreme Court formulations provide at once a doctrinal hook for litigants to use in advancing their claims and a language of rights that gives their doctrinal arguments a normative appeal. We might say that decisional constitutional law is both instrumentally useful and normatively supportive to rights claimants and political advocates. This was true for the abolitionists, and it remained so later for litigants seeking to use habeas corpus on behalf of convicted defendants, wartime enemies, and "war on terror" detainees.

4

Federal Common Law, Legal Realism, and the Magna Carta Tradition

Constitutional Interpretation in the Early Twentieth Century

> If there were such a transcendental body of law outside of any particular State . . . the Courts of the United States might be right in using their independent judgment as to what it was. But there is no such body of law. The fallacy and illusion that I think exist consist in supposing that there is this outside thing to be found.
>
> Justice Oliver Wendell Holmes, dissenting in *Black and White Taxicab v. Brown and Yellow Taxicab* (1928)

The first half of the twentieth century witnessed, among other things, the decline of federal common law and the birth of the Legal Realism movement. On the surface, these two developments do not seem to bear much relation to one another. The first is a response to a particular question of civil procedure, while the second endeavors to explain how judges make law. Neither question appears, at first glance, to touch the topic of the Magna Carta's legacy. However, my purpose in this chapter is to connect these points. The rise and fall of the federal common law was not merely a dispute about choice of law but rather a set of interconnected struggles: between state and federal courts, courts and legislatures, pro-business and pro-union factions, and so forth. Moreover, as the epigraph to this chapter shows, the federal common law controversy was, to a significant extent, a dispute about the question of where law comes from: From written sources? From tradition? From judges' wisdom? The Legal Realists sought to answer that question by depicting law as an open system that is influenced by a range of forces. One of the legacies of the Realists' movement was to demystify the process of legal development by showing how that development takes place within a social, historical, and political context. A common law tradition based in the Magna Carta might seem at odds with such a contextualized understanding of the work that judges do. But it is important to keep in mind that Legal Realism *itself* was a reaction to an overtly partisan (in the sense of pro-business orientation) federal judiciary in the late nineteenth and early twentieth centuries. In a sense, the Realists —and, most particularly, Holmes—were trying to reclaim a certain part of the common law legacy by unlinking its development from the interests of a dominant social group. Coke's conception of common law reason, and the conception expressed by James Wilson in the constitutional period, relied on practical experience in a way that prefigures the Realists' pragmatism centuries later. And so when we ask about what common law means, in terms of its origins, development, or shaping forces, we are asking what role the Magna Carta and other influences have played at different points in time. It is not enough to say that common law is influential or important—because judges and lawyers have understood and applied the concept of common law differently through English and American legal history. It meant one thing to nineteenth-century federal judges, and another to Progressive jurists like Louis Brandeis, and still another to the Legal Realists. These disputes over law's meaning are connected both temporally and conceptually in the cases and scholarly works that will be explored in this chapter. Perceiving the connections, though, requires careful attention to the doctrinal and historical developments of the turn-of-the-century period.

Twenty-first-century observers of the Supreme Court are prone to commit the error of *presentism*. Having seen the Court outlaw de jure racial segregation in *Brown v. Board of Education*, protect reproductive privacy in *Roe v. Wade*, and rule on issues such as flag burning and same-sex marriage, we might ascribe to it an inherently progressive institutional character. We might assume that it has always acted to protect the individual rights of vulnerable Americans, but this assumption would be historically inaccurate. As Noah Feldman points out, it was only in 1954, when *Brown* was handed down, that "the Supreme Court came to be seen as rightly devoted to the protection of minorities."[1] *Brown* was not the first decision upholding the constitutional rights of a minority group or an individual rights claimant, of course. Rather, Feldman's point is that the Court's institutional identity solidified after 1954 so that it could be seen somewhat consistently as an institution fulfilling that role from then on. This change was due in part to the strength of the individual personalities of certain members of the Court during the 1940s and 1950s. Feldman vividly demonstrates the ways in which the constitutional vision, temperament, and personal circumstances of Justices Frankfurter, Jackson, Black, and Douglas converged to produce the justices' votes and the unanimous opinion in *Brown*. Those votes, in turn, set the stage for future institutional and doctrinal developments on the Warren Court, which I will discuss in chapter 5. But there was a corresponding change in the institutional alignment of common law constitutionalism occurring around this same time, so that not only the Court's decisional output but also one of its main interpretive orientations underwent a fundamental shift. This chapter will describe the beginnings of these changes by focusing on events leading up to the watershed case of *Erie v. Tompkins* and then examining the *Erie* decision itself and its aftermath. In the course of considering *Erie* and its predecessors, it will be necessary to discuss the Legal Realism movement in legal thought and to outline the contributions to Legal Realism made by Holmes, Brandeis, and others. Thus, I will trace two broad trends in legal thought: (1) the rejection of "federal common law" as something that federal judges could discover, and (2) the acknowledgment (via Legal Realism) that law's development is open to, and shaped by, a range of social and political forces. As the civil rights movement gained force in the 1950s, the Supreme Court drew on a form of common law–influenced legal theory while at the same time distancing itself from the earlier conception of common law that the federal courts had been employing in the nineteenth and early twentieth centuries. In both periods, the Court was a powerful force in relation to the legislative and executive branches, but it spoke with a different voice as it moved from one phase to another. Though it is employed differently, the Magna Carta tradition can be seen in both phases.

The Conservatism of the Common Law

In the late nineteenth and early twentieth centuries, the common law was not seen as an instrument of progressive social change. Instead, it was associated with preserving the status quo. The common law stood in opposition to legislative initiatives promoting health and safety, and its advocates included federal judges and lawyers representing industry. Common law followed tradition, and tradition opposed change. Federal judges held that the accumulated wisdom of precedent and the strength of judicial reasoning should trump positive law enacted by reformist state lawmakers. Federal common law was a means for asserting power over progressive forces in the legislature and protecting existing configurations of power. Edward Purcell summarizes this institutional alignment as follows: "Corporate interests increasingly relied on the courts as their ultimate bulwark against regulatory action, and Progressives increasingly identified them with social conservatism, corporate power, and the protection of private property."[2] This conservative orientation has an air of elitism about it. Judges protecting interests and values against modernizing change were operating from a position of expertise, even wisdom. It is not difficult to see how the claims of judicial expertise propounded by Sir Edward Coke in the seventeenth century could generate such an attitude of elitism in the judicial establishment centuries later. The special training, temperament, and reasoning processes belonging to members of the bench enabled them to perceive and rebuff threats to the reason-based legal order. Threats came from popular movements within and outside state legislatures.

The infamous case of *Lochner v. New York* (1905)[3] is a good illustration of a legal dispute that reflects these larger tensions. *Lochner* involved a challenge to a New York law limiting bakers' working hours. The law was aimed at ameliorating the adverse health effects of bakery work. In this well-known decision, the Supreme Court invalidated the state law on the grounds that it interfered with the fundamental right to make a contract. Justice Holmes criticized the majority in *Lochner*, as did many other commentators afterward, for basing its decision on a popular doctrine of the time (laissez-faire capitalism). The case pitted progressive forces within the state legislature seeking to improve working conditions against industry lawyers fighting to preserve the supply of wage labor and to keep wages down. In that sense the interests in the case lined up as I have described earlier: the Supreme Court sided with bakery owners against wage laborers and struck down remedial legislation by relying on an unwritten rule that it found to be "higher" than legislative enactment.

Lochner was the first case to explicitly adopt the doctrine of "substantive due process," which recognizes certain fundamental interests that cannot be abridged by government action. "Due process" is a term that appears twice in the Constitution: in the Fifth Amendment, which was adopted as part of the Bill of

Rights in 1787, and in the Fourteenth Amendment, which was adopted after the Civil War. As explained in chapter 3, "due process of law" is understood as equivalent to the "law of the land" phraseology of the Magna Carta. Just as the Magna Carta proclaimed that no one (in government) will deprive a person of liberty or "go against" them except by the "law of the land," the Due Process Clause states that no one will be deprived of life, liberty, or property without due process of law. In the *Murray's Lessee* case discussed in chapter 3, Justice Curtis expounded on the meaning of due process and connected it to the common law and to the Magna Carta. When Curtis was writing in 1856, the phrase "substantive due process" was not in use. Due process was not qualified or modified in any way. But by the turn of the century, courts began to use the adjective "substantive" to emphasize the *nature* of the deprivation rather than the procedures followed to accomplish it. Some rights are so fundamental, in this way of thinking, that the government should never, or almost never, interfere with them. Later, legal scholars would delineate "procedural" due process alongside the substantive version when referring to the specific procedures (e.g., notice, hearing) required prior to an adverse action by the government against a person. Later, too, substantive due process would be applied to protect privacy in a range of settings: use of contraception, reproductive decisions, and intimate relationships. In 1905, though, the *Lochner* court adopted the substantive due process theory urged by the plaintiffs and invalidated the wage and hour law, to the benefit of New York bakery owners.

At the turn of the century, lawyers representing business interests in the courts were seeking to develop a new legal theory to protect property rights. In the early to mid-nineteenth century, the "Contracts Clause" of the Constitution had been used in several prominent cases to protect property rights. The Contracts Clause, Article I, Section 10, provides that "no state shall . . . pass any . . . law impairing the Obligation of Contracts."

In *Fletcher v. Peck* (1810),[4] the Marshall Court had to construe the Contracts Clause as it resolved a property dispute. It used the Contracts Clause to protect investors' rights, ruling that state law could not invalidate land purchases made by private parties even if the sellers in those transactions had acted fraudulently to obtain the land they later sold. Similarly, in *Sturges v. Crowninshield*,[5] the Court overturned, on the same grounds, a state bankruptcy law that would have discharged preexisting debts so that creditors could not recover them. These decisions gave business interests a legal theory with which to challenge unfavorable laws. A law that harmed their prospects could be described as an unconstitutional interference with contract rights. The rulings assumed a natural right to freedom of contract. However, by the mid-nineteenth century, the Supreme Court began to recognize that the "public good" (for example, the construction of a bridge) could sometimes outweigh the importance of contractual rights held by private parties. In other words, the Contracts Clause had become, by the mid-1800s, less of a sure thing for litigants asserting property rights. Pro-business lawyers needed a new theory of constitutional property rights, and they turned to the Due Process Clause to develop it. The Supreme Court gradually warmed to the substantive due process theory, and it endorsed it definitively in *Lochner*. Legislation that limited the ability to make contracts—that is, interfered with the fundamental liberty of contract—would violate the Due Process Clause.

The obvious question arising at this juncture is a methodological one. How can the Court justify reading a term into the constitutional text that is not explicit but that nonetheless shapes constitutional meaning in a fundamental way? Substantive due process in general and *Lochner* in particular are products of common law constitutionalism. The fundamental liberty of contract is a concept that was discussed by Locke and Blackstone, but it is not enumerated among specific guarantees of liberty contained in the Bill of Rights. Warrant for recognizing this right lies in custom and tradition, but not in the language of the Constitution. The ruling became controversial because it seemed to enshrine contemporary popular opinion as constitutional doctrine. It substituted public opinion for the specialized reason of the common law. As a result, not only the turn-of the-century Supreme Court but also the enterprise of common law constitutionalism itself became suspect.

Federal Common Law and Swift v. Tyson

Of course, the *Lochner* ruling did not materialize out of thin air. It shares a pro–federal court orientation with another aspect of federal court jurisprudence of the same time period: the ascendancy of federal common law as a basis for court decision making that was first established in *Swift v. Tyson* (1842).[6] Just as the common law constitutionalism of *Lochner* tipped the institutional balance in favor of federal courts and pro-industry lawyers, so did federal common law empower the federal judiciary at the expense of the states. Henry Hart and Herbert Wechsler define federal common law as "federal rules of decision where the authority for a federal rule is not explicitly found in federal statutory or constitutional command."[7] Under the Constitution's Supremacy Clause, federal law incorporated in the U.S. Constitution or the U.S. Code (federal statutes) would trump state law in the event of a conflict. But what law should be applied in cases not governed by federal statute or constitution? Did the law of the states include state court precedential decisions, or could the federal courts apply a general common law derived from the federal courts? If they could apply general common law, the federal courts would necessarily become more powerful because they could pick and choose the elements of this law they were fashioning; they would be free of state-law constraints that dictated results the federal courts did not want.

Swift v. Tyson was a commercial law dispute, involving negotiable instruments, that arose in New York. Plaintiff Swift filed a complaint in federal court based on diversity jurisdiction.[8] The trial court had to determine, first, which body of law would govern the dispute. New York State court decisions were inconclusive, but federal decisions favored the plaintiff. The Rules of Decision Act, which was part of the Judiciary Act of 1789, declared that unless federal treaty, statute, or constitutional provision applied to a given case, "the laws of the several states" must be applied by the federal courts in "trials at common law." Thus, the court had to define "the laws of the several states" as it proceeded to choose the governing law in the case. Was the common law of the State of New York, which had developed through the decisions of its state courts, to be considered "law" within the meaning of the Rules of Decision Act? The Supreme Court, in a decision written by Justice Story, said no. It decided that state case law was not part of "the laws of the several states." Story explained: "In the ordinary use of language it can hardly be contended that the decisions of courts constitute laws. They are, at most, only evidence of what the laws are, and are not of themselves laws."[9] With this pronouncement, the majority freed itself from the requirements of the Rules of Decision Act and proceeded to decide the case under "general principles and doctrines." Although this "general" law was in a strict sense the federal common law because it was developed and applied by the federal courts including the Supreme Court, it was subject to quite a bit of variation, since the federal courts were in fact free to choose the law they wished to apply. Given this discretion entrusted by the *Swift* decision to federal judges, there could be a wide range of "general principles and doctrines" subsumed under the heading of "federal common law."

It is crucial to note the assumption underlying the claim that court decisions are "evidence of what the laws are" rather than laws themselves. The claim suggests that laws themselves are there to be discovered. Like a treasure or an unknown species of bird, law understood this way exists independently of those who are searching for it; it is an "outside thing." This assumption contrasts sharply with the notion that laws are *made*. In *Swift*, the Court gravitates to the first assumption (i.e., that law is found), which puts the Supreme Court in a privileged epistemic position as compared with the state courts because the Court can find the "right answer" from among the available alternatives, and that answer will be objectively correct. Such a conception is of course quite serviceable for a Court with the institutional orientation I have described earlier. If the Court sees its proper role as facilitating certain political outcomes, such as the expansion of interstate commerce and the prosperity of business interests, that role is easier to fulfill once the Court is free to choose among alternative theories and select the one most conducive to those outcomes. It need not defer to state court decisional law that might frustrate attempts to reach the results determined in advance to be best. Also, the epistemic position allowed by the assumption that law is discovered rather than made dovetails nicely with the image of the Court as guardian of age-old wisdom. We have seen again and again, through the common law history recounted here, how judges often claim for themselves a unique and special expertise in applying the common law. Sometimes, this age-old wisdom emanated from venerable texts such as the Magna Carta.

Purcell notes that Justice Brewer was a particularly forceful proponent of federal common law who also exhibited a commitment to the "superior wisdom" view I have just outlined. For Brewer, it was true that business interests were important to society's development and that interstate commerce deserved the support of the courts, but Brewer's outlook was also explicitly based on a particular moral view. A devout Christian, Brewer saw the federal courts, and the Supreme Court in particular, as guardians of a moral order resting on social stratification and adherence to principle. Viewed this way, Brewer's belief that the federal courts should act to support business interests is strengthened by religious beliefs that tend to the same effect. His worldview envisioned a nation whose courts would closely watch over its moral development and also generate a business-oriented legal system. As Purcell characterizes Brewer's outlook, "The nation confronted grave dangers, and only the courts could save it. Government centralization, political demagoguery, labor unions, greedy legislatures, and non-Anglo-Saxon races threatened to disrupt American society and destroy its institutions."[10] In terms of constitutional authority, Brewer looked to "the fact that it incorporated the principles of the Declaration of Independence and the divine truths of Christianity."[11] Purcell notes the application of these beliefs in several key majority opinions authored by Brewer. In *Baltimore and Ohio Railroad v. Baugh* (1893),[12] he applied federal common law to industrial tort law in a ruling that favored employer-defendants over employee-plaintiffs. In *Kansas v. Colorado*,[13] Brewer asserted the authority of federal common law over an interstate water use dispute. It was not surprising that the federal government would be empowered to make rules in this area. What *was* surprising was Brewer's assertion that only the federal courts, rather than Congress or the executive, could make rules in this area. And in *In re Debs*,[14] he asserted the power of the federal courts, via federal common law, to end labor disputes. Again, these decisions expanded the reach of the federal common law, as determined by the federal courts, over areas where state courts, or the coordinate branches of the federal government, had tried to assert authority. The federal courts were thus empowered to discover common law truths accessible only to them, and then to apply those truths on the side of certain interests, particularly economic corporations.

Thus, in the wake of *Swift v. Tyson*, federal courts became increasingly free to apply federal common law (i.e., common law of their own determining) in other contexts outside the context of the law of negotiable instruments that was at issue in *Swift* itself.

One result of this development was that litigants could manipulate legal process for strategic advantage. Plaintiffs could utilize the federal forum in order to avoid the unfavorable common law of the state, and defendants could remove cases to federal court for the same reason. There is nothing immediately wrong with choosing a forum strategically, of course. The concern that developed, rather, was over the extent to which this was done. In *Black and White Taxicab and Transfer Co. v. Brown and Yellow Taxicab and Transfer Co.*, the Court allowed a striking degree of manipulation.[15] The plaintiff, a Kentucky corporation, moved to Tennessee in order to be able to sue in federal court under diversity jurisdiction and avoid application of Kentucky case law. In fact, as Charles Wright notes, "The reincorporation in Tennessee in order to create diversity verged on fraud, and it was not necessary to hold that diversity jurisdiction could be so readily abused."[16] Nonetheless, the Court ruled in favor of the plaintiff, in effect rewarding the corporation for its questionable use of diversity jurisdiction. The line of state court decisions favoring the defendant was rejected as authority by the Court because they were "contrary to the common law as generally understood and applied."[17]

Holmes dissented, with Brandeis and Stone joining him. He saw this case as an unwarranted expansion of the *Swift* doctrine into a new area. His main concern was the Court's disregarding of state sovereignty. This was a case arising in Kentucky, concerning property law in Kentucky. As such, "The voice adopted by the State as its own should utter the last word."[18] It was improper, he thought, to resort to other authorities to decide the matter. But Holmes also spoke more generally about the nature of law. The majority had superimposed a universally applicable common law on the common law of the state, and Holmes doubted the existence of such law. He wrote, "If there were such a transcendental body of law outside of any particular State . . . the Courts of the United States might be right in using their independent judgment as to what it was. But there is no such body of law. The fallacy and illusion that I think exist consist in supposing that there is this outside thing to be found."[19] This statement reveals Holmes's belief that all law proceeds from a sovereign and requires the lawmaking authority that a sovereign possesses. This belief forms a basis for Holmes's legal positivism and distinguishes him from legal thinkers who thought that law was found rather than made. It is important to note that Holmes had his own conception of the common law and that he did not reject the idea of the common law as invalid in itself; he simply differed on its origins. Later in this chapter, I will reexamine Holmes's views on the common law in the context of the Legal Realism movement. First, though, it is necessary to explain how and why the court overturned *Swift* in 1938, nearly a century after it was decided.

Erie Railroad Co. v. Tompkins *Overturns* Swift

Federal courts continued to face the dilemma posed by *Swift* and revisited in *Black and White Taxicab* and other cases. The question was

> whether in "filling in" the interstices and gaps left open by federal statutory regulation, or in interpreting general statutes or phrases, the federal courts should fashion federal "common law" or should resort to state law. And note that this question shades into—and is often indistinguishable from—the pervasive question of the extent to which federal regulation displaces or preempts preexisting law within (and adjacent to) the field of federal regulation.[20]

As the Court consistently indicated that federal courts should make common law that replaced state law, the scope of the preemption widened, and extreme examples of forum-shopping like the one in *Black and White Taxicab* continued to occur.

By the early 1930s, criticisms of *Swift* were mounting. For one thing, it was apparent that a system where federal courts could select applicable law from among alternatives often produced results that were difficult to predict in advance and highly inconsistent, and therefore "rendered impossible equal protection of the laws."[21] Justice Brandeis seized the opportunity in 1938 to finally overrule *Swift* when a tort suit came before the Court involving an accident on a railroad right-of-way in Pennsylvania. Ironically, the party seeking to avoid unfavorable state common law was not a business corporation but an individual, Harry Tompkins, who had lost his arm in the accident. The lawyer for the Erie Railroad Co. was thus placed in the position of having to argue against the rule in *Swift v. Tyson*, which had so often been useful to the railroad companies and other business concerns. Purcell shows convincingly that counsel for Erie avoided suggesting that *Swift* should be overturned, resting his defense on other grounds instead.[22] Nonetheless, at oral argument the Court posed the question of overturning Swift to counsel for the parties, and that became the basis for deciding the case.

Writing for the majority, Brandeis announced the new interpretation of the Rules of Decision Act that rejected the notion of federal common law: "Except in matters governed by the federal constitution or by acts of Congress, the law to be applied in any case is the law of the state. And whether the law of the state shall be declared by its legislature in a statute or by its highest court in a decision is not a matter of federal concern."[23] In explaining why federal common law was being displaced in favor of the decisional law of the state courts, Brandeis utilized Holmes's positivist argument. Law flowed from a sovereign and was not discovered but made, whether by legislatures or courts empowered by the government of the states. Brandeis quoted Holmes: "The common law so far as it is enforced in a state, whether called common law or not, is not the common law generally but the law of that state existing by the authority of that state without regard to what it may have been in England or anywhere else."[24]

This view that law must proceed from a sovereign had been advanced by other commentators in the years preceding *Erie*. John Chipman Gray made the point by comparing countries that follow a common law tradition to countries that do not follow that tradition. In England and the United States, judges are empowered by the sovereign to interpret the law, and by that grant of power their decisions have binding force. In Germany, because judges lacked that power, they did not make law.[25] Thus, Chipman Gray argued, what judges decide in the common law tradition is not merely evidence of law but rather law itself. He demonstrates this claim by comparing common law to the laws of physics and finding an important difference between them. Physicists find ways to explain the motion of objects, but those objects exhibit motion *independently* of whether or not their motion is being described. As a result, it is possible to speak of the laws of physics as discoverable. The common law, by contrast, is law *because* judges pronounce it. Citing *McCulloch v. Maryland*, Chipman Gray notes that the decision in that case would have been *different law* if Chief Justice Marshall had "hated the United States Bank and loved Thomas Jefferson."[26] *McCulloch* was a constitutional decision that drew on common law methodology, and it established what the law would be regarding the constitutionality of the national bank, as well as the ability of the state of Maryland to tax it. Marshall's statement was not merely evidence of the law; it *was* the law. By this line of argument, Chipman Gray refuted Justice Story's claim in *Swift* that common law decisions were merely evidence of the law and nothing more. This criticism of *Swift v. Tyson* preceded *Erie v. Tompkins* by two decades, but it captured the Realists' emphasis on practical results in jurisprudence as well as their rejection of a priori bodies of law that exist independently of human design or intention.

Given the critiques of *Swift* already in existence by 1938, there were ample resources from which Brandeis could draw in crafting his opinion in *Erie*, and much of this material came from the Realist camp. But what drew Brandeis to the Realist perspective in the first place? It cannot be overlooked that Brandeis' *Erie* opinion is consistent with his views about the balance of power between state and federal government, as well as his view as to how law should function in a society. Brandeis favored allowing the states to experiment with legislation that ameliorated social ills. As a trial lawyer, he had famously defended an Oregon statute limiting working hours for laundry workers, providing voluminous social science data to support his position.[27] And he openly expressed concern about the effects of private economic power on individuals. Thus, the result reached in *Erie* very much fit with his own preferences.[28] As Purcell describes Brandeis, "Antagonism toward corporate concentration was a cornerstone of Brandeis' philosophy. 'Bigness' was the central evil, and national corporations represented the most dominant form of bigness in twentieth century America . . . they defeated the hopes of small and mortal individuals."[29] Later, disputes would arise over the true meaning of *Erie* in ideological terms, as Frankfurter and others fought to claim Brandeis's Progressive legacy. Was the decision a statement against corporate dominance of the legal system, or an affirmation of principled, restrained, and deferential judicial behavior?

Was the *Erie* case simply a matter of interpreting a federal statute (Rules of Decision Act) correctly, or did it have a deeper foundation? Purcell shows that Brandeis wanted to emphasize the constitutional dimension of the ruling. As evidence, he cites Brandeis's early draft of the opinion where Brandeis says the result is required by the Constitution.[30] And it appears that in negotiations with the majority coalition that signed the opinion,

Brandeis was encouraged to include some constitutional references that we see in the published opinion. And yet, as Purcell notes, Brandeis *avoided* mentioning the Tenth Amendment, which would have obliged him to address the topic of reserved powers. The Tenth Amendment provides that powers not granted to the federal government are reserved to the states or the people. This was not territory Brandeis wanted to cover; it would have complicated the opinion without strengthening its pro-states thrust appreciably.

Nonetheless, subsequent commentary has emphasized the constitutional dimensions of the case. An early American Law Institute (ALI) report affirms that *Erie* is based in the Constitution. *Erie*, the ALI states, "is of constitutional dimension in the sense that it rests upon premises related to the basic nature of our federal system and produces a pattern of results more in accord with that system, under current conceptions of law, than the required rule of custom."[31] One way to read this statement is to focus on Article III of the Constitution, which gives the federal courts their institutional powers. To nullify the power and effect of state courts, as the federal common law rule in *Swift* had done, would be to read the Article III grant of judicial power far too expansively. Moreover, if the federal government is one of enumerated powers, as has been so often stated, then each assertion of power by one of its branches must be traced to what is expressed or implied in the Constitution. The result in *Erie* affirms these premises and thus touches on the subject of constitutional powers. The federal courts could not devise federal common law in order to avoid undesirable state common law, and this limitation was rooted in the Constitution itself.

This change in the Supreme Court's orientation vis-à-vis the common law functioned as a course correction by limiting the ability of the federal courts to "discover" legal principles to override state court decisional law. This course correction was especially significant because federal judges had largely been using the "discovery" approach to favor business interests over individual rights since the time of *Swift v. Tyson*. The federal judges' assertion of a special ability to employ common law reason did not preclude their use of ancient sources of law, but clearly the Magna Carta's Article 39 was not always an appealing or useful one. Article 39's emphasis on individual rights against state power would not always help to promote the interests the Court was favoring at the turn of the century. However, sometimes it did. Economic substantive due process, as established in *Lochner* and other cases, did in fact empower the individual to resist state regulation. All in all, it was often results more than principle that led the Court to its interpretive choices during this period, and as Brandeis and other saw this, they urged reform.

The Legal Realism Movement

Legal Realism developed in reaction to the formalism and institutional aggrandizement exemplified by Supreme Court decisions such as *Swift* and *Lochner*. As I have shown here, both of those rulings rested on assumptions of federal court superiority. In the first place, they claimed a privileged role for the federal courts—by denying effect to the decisions of state courts (in *Swift*) and overturning the enactments of a state legislature (in *Lochner*). In addition, both decisions shared a formalistic methodology. Both courts assumed that objective principles of law could be discovered by judges applying common law reasoning according to their own lights. Getting to the right answer in a dispute between litigants involved an abstract reasoning process that was not influenced in any way by politics, sociology, class position, economics, or any other factor. To some, this was a false objectivity. Justice Holmes's dissent in *Lochner* pointed out that the ruling actually implemented a specific policy view under the guise of an abstract and objective principle. "The Fourteenth

Amendment does not enact Mr. Herbert Spencer's Social Statics," he wrote.[32] This was an early example of judicial opposition to formalism, and Holmes was one of the most influential voices to sound that antiformalist refrain. He rearticulated the enterprise of interpreting the common law as an *inquiry*. What we want to know most, he said, is what judges will do with future cases, and in making such "prophecies" students and other observers of law draw on past experience and present trends. Rather than abandoning the common law, then, Holmes wanted to view it in a different way. The history of the common law is important to know because it enables the student or litigant to make better prophecies, but history and tradition by themselves do not furnish sufficient reason to adhere to a common law rule.

It is useful to start with Justice Holmes when attempting to reconstruct the project of the Legal Realists. Holmes's judicial career began before Realism and continued into the period when Realism was in full swing. All along, Holmes urged a critical attitude toward custom, tradition, and history in relation to law, though he acknowledged the importance of being aware of them. As Holmes wrote in "The Path of the Law," "The rational study of law is still to a large extent the study of history. History must be a part of the study, because without it we cannot know the precise scope of rules which it is our business to know."[33] But he strongly opposed unreflective adherence to tradition. Often rules were followed simply out of habit born of tradition, and this was anathema to Holmes's pragmatic outlook. Pragmatism in philosophy was one of the developments in early twentieth-century learning that catalyzed the Realists, and Holmes was influential to American pragmatism as well as to legal thought.[34] Holmes's pragmatism keyed him to the importance of experience while also leading him to emphasize the practical consequences of judicial rulings. In one of his most-quoted statements, he says in *The Common Law*, "The life of the law has not been logic; it has been experience."[35] This focus on practical results and the willingness to experiment in order to obtain those results form one of the legacies of Holmes's powerful personality on twentieth-century legal thought.

Related to the emphasis on practical consequences, Holmes urged judges to "consider more definitely and explicitly the social advantage on which the rule they lay down must be justified."[36] Judges who saw themselves simply applying the results of a logical exercise would miss the effects of their rulings on actual people. And because people are positioned differently in society, possessing differing degrees of "social advantage," this kind of decisional myopia could work to the long- and short-term harm of the parties before the court, and in the larger society. Holmes's practical focus, by contrast, would sometimes make judges "hesitate where they are now confident."[37] Roscoe Pound, a legal scholar who shared early affinities with the Realists but later criticized them, termed this kind of willful blindness to consequences "mechanical jurisprudence."[38] Judges interpreted the Constitution in an artificial way, Pound believed, when they sought logically perfect and objectively correct formulations that would solve problems in jurisprudence once and for all. "Mechanical" suggests a process that unfolds without deliberate thought, while "artificial" brings to mind a staged or contrived event that does not reflect real-world conditions. Though Pound later faulted the Realists for such things as overreliance on statistical data, his critique of mechanical jurisprudence set forth in "Liberty of Contract" (1909) effectively captures what troubled the Realists and their sympathizers about late nineteenth-century and early twentieth-century classical legal thought.

The critique of formalism in classical legal thought was in part a critique of natural law. As we have seen, the common law tradition originating in England and relying on the Magna Carta's declaration of liberty was often linked with natural law. In the slavery cases, courts connected the common law tradition of freedom to natural law as they proclaimed slavery as contrary to that tradition. Common law liberty and natural law lined up on one side, and "municipal" or statutory law stood on the other side of the line: natural law prohibited slavery, and positive law authorized it. Writing in 1909, Pound could perceive that natural law theories still held sway in legal thought despite the scientific turn in the social sciences. In fact, Pound noted, "constitutional law is full of natural law notions. For one thing, there is the doctrine that apart from constitutional restrictions there are individual rights resting on a natural basis, to which courts must give effect 'beyond the control of the state.'" And, in practice, "this feeling operates in constitutional law to lead judges to try statutes by the measure of common law doctrines rather than by the Constitution."[39] In a separate treatise, Pound asserts, "Our bills of rights are regarded as merely declaratory of fundamental natural rights. Eminent justices assert that legislation is to be judged by those rights and not by the constitutional texts in which they are declared."[40] He is describing common law constitutionalism here, and he finds it to be misguided. By adhering to common law constitutionalism, he thought, judges were approaching legal problems in a way that no longer made sense, and in fact opened up a gulf between social justice and legal justice. We could say that "social justice" refers to collective claims for material resources and esteem made by groups in a pluralistic society, while "legal justice" refers to judgments that conform to an ideal reflected in a fixed conception of right. This formulation is keenly insightful and valuable, for it captures the divergence between the emerging politics of the new century (along with the social science used to describe it) and the classical legal thought that judges persistently applied despite the changing world around them.

However, developments later in the century made it possible to speak of a new synthesis between social and legal justice. Some of the claims brought by marginalized social groups could be described as claims for legal justice. In particular, legal challenges to racial segregation were premised on the idea of human equality. Equality of persons, as John Rawls would say later, was a fundamental principle of justice claimed by liberalism, sometimes based in natural law, and also declared in constitutional text. The discussion of specific desegregation cases during the Warren years, which is contained in chapter 5, will examine this synthesis more fully, but it bears mentioning here as a challenge to the critique of common law constitutionalism posed by Pound.

Later, Pound would criticize the Realists for, among other things, excessive reliance on "faith in masses of figures as having significance in and of themselves."[41] He also perceived an overreliance on social science in general on the Realists' part. It must be noted that this science-related complaint was quite different from the attack on the natural law–based universalism of the classical legal thought that preceded the Realists and showed forth in *Swift v. Tyson*. In that earlier mode of thought, the claim was that federal judges could discern universal and objective truths in the law by virtue of the judges' superior wisdom and perception. They were thus freed from the strictures of state court–created common law that they did not like. Pound's attack on the Realists, by contrast, stemmed from his view that social and behavioral science threatened, in the hands of the Realists, to displace entirely the use of conceptual analysis in law. Pound warned that statistics, or depth psychology, would presume to explain legal outcomes so that there would be no attention to rules. Thus Pound occupied a pivotal place in the history of legal thought, for he criticized the classical jurisprudence of the late nineteenth century for ignoring "law in action," but he also found the Realists' critiques of that same jurisprudence to be too extreme. One lesson to take from Pound's detailed position is that Realism was not a monolithic view. In fact, according to Pound's interlocutor Karl Llewellyn, Realism was not a school of thought at all but a series of departing points for modern legal inquiry.

In the early 1930s, Llewellyn engaged in a high-visibility debate with Pound over the nature and the value of Legal Realism. Here, Llewellyn characterized Pound as "a man partially caught in the traditional precept-thinking of an age that is passing"—a sharp and rather interesting attack considering the importance of Pound's earlier work to Legal Realism itself.[42] But Llewellyn sought to clarify where he thought Realism was going, and he did so in two steps. First, he emphasized the diversity of views held by individual Realists by actually *counting* the theorists associated with each of the claims Pound was criticizing. By this demonstration, Llewellyn showed not only variety but disagreement among the Realists so that it would be difficult to make blanket statements about the movement. Second, Llewellyn did list and briefly describe "common points of departure" for members of the movement. Prominent among those points was the "distrust of traditional legal rules and concepts in so far as they purport to describe what either courts or people are actually doing."[43] This "distrust of traditional legal rules" is significant. It stakes out a ground of skepticism beyond where the pragmatists were willing to go. More than tying a rule to practical utility, the Realists venture to say that rules are misleading because they create an illusory link between intention and apparent result. Rather than declaring a necessary and objectively correct result, the rule applied in a case could reward the party with greater economic power, as "liberty of contract" did in *Lochner*. Sometimes, judges might apply legal rules consciously as a "cover" for protection of class interest, but things were not always so straightforward. In many cases, what courts are "actually doing" might not depend on judges' intentions. What they are actually doing might be better explained by the *function* of their decision making and analysis. A ruling affects the balance of power among governmental branches; it creates incentives and disincentives for future parties in their commercial interactions; it shapes future litigation in terms of the types of cases that will be brought. This functional description, with its disjunction between rules and judicial behavior, can subsume within it a range of articulations of Realism, from Jerome Frank's psychological analysis of law as paternal authority,[44] to Herman Oliphant's call for replacing the "intuitive empiricism" of the past with a turn to the social sciences in recognition of a thicker social reality.[45]

This is not the place to referee the dispute between the Realists and their critics. Nonetheless, some observations about Realism in relation to common law constitutionalism are in order. The quarrel over Realism bears a similarity to a later one over the social theory of Michel Foucault. Like the Realists, Foucault made important descriptive insights that profoundly affected the subsequent study of social phenomena. And like the Realists, Foucault suffered from what Nancy Fraser has called "normative confusion."[46] He left us no clear basis for saying what institutions or practices were preferable to the ones he described as existent, much less an indication of how to attain them. To the extent that Foucault supported practical action, it seemed to be atomized, nonprogrammatic resistance to power. Yet no one would deny the effect that his use of genealogy and discourse analysis has had on multiple disciplines, not only within the social sciences but also in the humanities. The Realists were similarly influential. Their critique changed legal thought by imbuing it with an enduring skepticism about rules. And when the Critical Legal Studies movement got started in the 1970s, the connections to Realism were explicitly affirmed as well as readily observable. The validity of particular criticisms of Legal Realism seems far less interesting or significant, a century later, than the fact that a number of Realism's tenets have become commonplace assumptions in the study of law.

But what of constitutionalism? While some of the Realists' work was directed at private law, they addressed constitutional law as well.[47] And some of their work has application in both public and private domains. For instance, in one of his less bold formulations, Llewellyn cited the "need for courts to face squarely the policy questions in their cases, and to use the full freedom precedent affords in working towards conclusions that seem indicated."[48] Here was a directive aimed not at commentators but rather at those entrusted with making law. Llewellyn echoes Holmes by calling for forthright acknowledgment of the policy dimension of judicial decision making, and he also urges a flexible attitude toward precedent, implying that it is indeterminate rather than fixed. These precepts could be accommodated within a conception of common law constitutionalism, though such a conception would diverge from the nineteenth-century version. Frankness about policy concerns and flexibility toward precedent have come to be commonplace among many of the twentieth-century (and twenty-first-century) justices. In this regard, a specific element of the Realist project can claim a legacy in contemporary constitutional interpretation. It can be said, then, that Realism's imprint on legal thought is discernible in the general and the specific.

Additionally, Llewellyn charged that Pound was overly fuzzy in his articulation of "custom" as a source of decisional influence.[49] If judges could legitimately draw upon custom as part of their decision-making methodology, it was necessary to specify what is meant by custom. This is a problem in common law constitutionalism more generally, and it raises some questions. What counts as custom? Are all forms of custom persuasive and legitimate sources of authority? Are they ranked somehow in terms of persuasive force, or are they all equal? Must custom be validated legally or politically before it can be applied as a decisional ground? From the Realist perspective, the question becomes one of the force of custom on the judicial enterprise rather than the validity of customary rules because the Realists are not looking to ground or validate legal rules. Instead, they want to account for legal outcomes. But there is some common ground. Holmes wrote in *The Common Law* of "history" and "the felt necessities of the time"; Pound makes reference to custom; Llewellyn urged "working toward the conclusions that seem indicated." All of them share a sense that at least part of the time there are resolutions possible that draw on precedent in a sound way and consequently come to serve as guiding precedent for future courts. Noah Feldman describes Justice Jackson's concurrence in *Youngstown Sheet and Tube Co. v. Sawyer* that way.[50] When President Truman ordered seizure of the nation's steel mills during the Korean War, the Court had to decide whether the president possessed the power to take such an action. The Court decided that Truman did not have the power to do so, and Jackson wrote a concurrence that has stood as a powerful and persuasive analysis of presidential power. Jackson's opinion provided a framework of three categories of presidential action, each of which carried with it a warrant for action. When the president acts in conflict with the will of Congress, the warrant is weakest, or "at its lowest ebb." Truman's steel seizure fell within the third category and was therefore invalid. Jackson wrote squarely within the bounds of previous analyses of presidential power, but he also infused his opinion with a form of pragmatism that made it both wise and useful. It is still respected—and cited widely—today. This pragmatic element serves as a criterion for judging constitutional precedent, not as the expression of eternal truths but rather as well-reasoned decisions that reflect and respond to the "felt necessities of the time." Pragmatism is certainly not the only legacy of the Realists, or even the most characteristic one, but it does inform constitutional tradition in a lasting way.

Conclusion: Federal Common Law after Erie

This chapter has traced constitutional jurisprudence through the late nineteenth and early twentieth centuries, focusing on the dominant role during that time of the federal courts in American legal development. This dominance is reflected in the Court's establishment of federal common law as superior to the common law of the states in federal court litigation. This allowed the federal courts, including the Supreme Court, to apply rules of decision of their own choosing in a wide range of matters that came before them. The practice was of constitutional significance in the sense that it marked a new division of state versus federal power. Epistemically, the reliance on federal common law reflected the belief that universal law existed independently of governmental act and could be discovered by those with the requisite wisdom and discernment (which meant only the federal courts).

This state of things continued until 1938, when Justice Brandeis authored the *Erie* opinion. *Erie* restored state common law precedent as the rules of decision to be used in federal court cases where federal statute or constitution did not apply. This adjustment moved state-federal relations in the direction of greater state control, and it also put an end to some of the blatant and egregious forum-shopping that litigants (particularly corporate litigants) had engaged in under the old rule. Thus, *Erie* itself was a reorientation of constitutional jurisprudence that gave recognition to state sovereignty and rejected the superior position that had been claimed by the federal judiciary and some members of the legal establishment at the expense of the states and the people.

It is important to specify what is left, post-*Erie*, of federal common law (i.e., the power of the federal courts to generate common law). One way to do this is to explore two questions: First, what space did *Erie* leave for federal courts to develop a body of decisional law? Second, what has been the effect of time on the rule announced in *Erie*? As to the first question, we must first bear in mind that the precise holding simply limited federal courts from choosing which body of decisional law to apply in diversity actions coming before it. In matters of common law, the case law of the state would control, and the federal courts would have to apply it. In instances where federal statute or constitutional provisions were in issue, *Erie* did not apply, of course.

But things are not as simple as making a dividing line between statute and common law. For as Louise Weinberg points out, "In all cases along the continuum courts obviously glean what they can from legislative action or inaction."[51] The reach of a particular statute may be one of the contested issues in a case, or the legislature may have taken some action in a given field of regulation without occupying the field entirely. Either way, there will be some statutory scheme, some "kernel" of text,[52] that could bear on the case, or the *lack* of legislation could be taken to indicate the legislature's position. Action or inaction, courts must decide what to make of that.

As for "constitutional common law," Weinberg finds that separate category to be similarly problematic because federal courts *always* have a theoretical override of legislative action available to them via judicial review.[53] Because courts have the power of judicial review, there is no need for a category of "constitutional common law" because all cases potentially involve constitutional common law. The blurry lines between statute/common law and constitution/statute indicate that the effect of *Erie* does not go so far as to foreclose all development of federal common law. Federal courts are faced perpetually with decisional imperatives that require them to negotiate limits of federalism and limits of deference to legislative will, and their rulings will inevitably raise questions about whether they have exceeded one set of bounds or the other. It has often been possible to chart the swings of the Supreme Court across time periods and to say that the Court expanded federal power at one point and contracted it at another. This is true not only of the span of time between *Swift* and *Erie* but also between the Warren and Rehnquist Courts. Writing in 1989, Weinberg perceived a general skepticism toward federal common law at that time.[54] And even within that pendular swing, she could pinpoint particular cases where conservative justices advocated federal common law and liberal ones bemoaned it.[55]

In order to tie this discussion of *Erie* and federal common law back to the question of common law constitutionalism, it is necessary to ask what effect the *Swift/Erie* chapter of constitutional jurisprudence has had on the common law orientation to interpreting the Constitution. The century-long episode described in this chapter has shown the harm that can result when an instrumental approach to law is masked as objective. Decisions favoring powerful groups in society appeared to draw on law derived, in Holmes's words, from a "brooding omnipresence in the sky" when in fact their effects were purposeful and particularistic.[56] But this fault should not discredit common law constitutionalism altogether. For the meaning of "common law" itself was changed in the transition from *Swift* to *Erie* and in the following years. Weinberg has pointed out that "in this country the 'common law' no longer means what it meant in eighteenth century England. The common law is not the law of general understandings, common to all English-speaking people. In the United States today, common law means judge-made law, in equity and criminal cases no less than in an actions at law. It is case law."[57] Constitutional case law continues to draw on earlier sources, including the Magna Carta. Yet the specific terms within its lexicon—the language of individual rights—continue to develop as new cases and controversies arise, so that their meanings are shaped by successive reinterpretations, as is the meaning of "common law" itself.

5

The Warren Court, Civil Rights, and the Incorporation Controversy

At the time the privilege of the writ [of habeas corpus] was written into the Federal Constitution it was settled that the writ lay to test any restraint contrary to fundamental law, which in England stemmed from Magna Charta but in this country was embodied in the written constitution.

JUSTICE BRENNAN IN *Fay v. Noia* (1963)

The Warren Court reoriented common law constitutionalism once again. The justices created decisional law that emphasized individual rights and also gave the Court a powerful role in protecting the rights of individuals. Sometimes the connections between this jurisprudence and the Magna Carta's promise of liberty were explicit, as in the epigraph to this chapter. In other instances, it is necessary to look beneath the surface of the legal language to perceive the Magna Carta's influence—as, for example, when the Court expanded due process in privacy cases. But no one would deny the influence of the Warren Court on individual rights, and no one would doubt that the "law of the land"/due process provision of the Magna Carta aided this development.

Earl Warren became chief justice in 1953 as the Supreme Court prepared to hear a second round of arguments in the desegregation cases consolidated under *Brown v. Board of Education*, and before the Court had rendered a decision in the cases. Warren served as chief justice from 1953 to 1969, during which time the Court announced its historic ruling in *Brown* and also issued numerous rulings in enforcement of *Brown*'s holding that state-enforced racial segregation of public schools violated the Fourteenth Amendment. In addition to the monumentally important equal protection precedent represented by *Brown*, the Warren Court's other principal legacies were its protection of voting rights and its incorporation of Bill of Rights provisions into the Fourteenth Amendment so that those provisions applied against the states as well as the federal government (for instance, *Mapp v. Ohio* established that evidence seized in violation of the Fourth Amendment was barred from use in state as well as federal criminal prosecutions). In these areas—equal protection, voting, and incorporation of the Bill of Rights—the Warren Court changed the course of constitutional interpretation in ways that broadened individual rights protections for vulnerable individuals and groups: African American students, speakers holding unpopular views, and criminal defendants, among others. Some viewed this "rights revolution" as an unprincipled and result-oriented expansion of judicial power. They believed that the Court's focus on justice for the groups mentioned earlier came at the expense of the institutional and doctrinal limits previously observed and also diminished the Court's integrity and legitimacy. Others—myself included—find the same developments to be salutary and readily explainable within the development of common law constitutionalism. I will argue in this chapter that the Warren Court continued key aspects of that tradition, particularly in its flexible application of precedent and its commitment to using constitutional concepts to promote equality as a deep social value. Some of the criticisms are misplaced, I will argue, because they rely on the assumptions of formalism that were discredited by the Legal Realists in the decades preceding Earl Warren's ascension to the bench. To require or expect courts to ignore the larger social consequences, or what Holmes called the "social advantage," of a particular ruling is a relic of the formalistic approach to legal analysis. As the Court construed the meaning of "equality" under the Fourteenth Amendment, for example, it took into account the effect of decades of Jim Crow laws and practices on black Americans. This broader perspective allowed the Court to outlaw segregated schools even though the history of the Fourteenth Amendment did not indicate that its passage was meant to do so.

The rights tradition of the Magna Carta can be seen lying behind the Warren Court's decisions, just as it provides a backdrop to the constitutional interpretive work of preceding justices. As noted in the last chapter, "common law" itself had come to acquire a different meaning in the twentieth century: rather than an amalgam of customary practices, its meaning had come to focus more sharply on case law.[1] In the Warren Court's establishment of new constitutional norms that have since become entrenched and unquestioned components of law, it is clear that common law, in an important sense, *is* case law: specifically, the precedents in equal protection, voting rights, criminal procedure, and civil liberties crafted by the Court in the 1950s and 1960s.

Justice William Brennan, an influential member of the Warren Court who remained on the Court for two decades after Warren retired, spoke often of the relationship between written and unwritten constitutional tradition. In the epigraph to this chapter, Brennan distinguishes English and American constitutionalism in this way. The written constitution was the source of law from which constitutional precedent would develop in our system. And yet Brennan believed that his role as justice required him to be responsive to the needs and problems of his time. He frequently affirmed his view of the Constitution as a living document that could be adapted to current conditions. Thus, his judicial opinions develop constitutional meaning through an interplay of written and unwritten sources, relying on what Amar calls "America's unwritten constitution." Brennan was forthright and unapologetic about this approach, and he found accountability in the "dialogue" that the Court conducted, over time, with the legislature.[2] Each time the Court rules in a particular case, Congress can respond by limiting or reversing that ruling through legislative action. Envisioning constitutional interpretation as a dialogue yields another understanding of the interrelationship of written and unwritten law: meaning is perpetually tested and contested, and the "unwritten" law of court opinions remains tied to the written law enacted by the legislature in a dialogical relationship.

This chapter will trace the development of common law constitutionalism during the Warren years by summarizing the case law generated during that period and exploring some of the critiques directed against the Court by prominent legal scholars such as Alexander Bickel and Henry Hart. Although the Magna Carta is mentioned by name only occasionally in the case law of this period, its influence will be clearly discernible as the Court seeks to reconcile past and present into a coherent and workable jurisprudence.

Racial Equality

Among lawyers and nonlawyers alike, the Warren Court is best known for its ruling in *Brown v. Board of Education*, which ended state-enforced racial segregation in public schools. The *Brown* ruling rested on the Equal Protection Clause of the Fourteenth Amendment, which provides, "No State shall . . . deny to any person within its jurisdiction the equal protection of the laws." In assessing the Warren Court's equal protection jurisprudence, it is important to note the uniqueness of the role the Court set for itself. As Feldman points out, "At no time in the history of the United States had a judicial body stood in the vanguard of progressive social change. For that matter, no judges in the world had ever done such a thing."[3] In 1954, it was clear that Congress would not act to end the state-enforced, racialized caste system then existing in public education and in the larger society. And yet the basic injustice of that system had been demonstrated by litigants coming before the Court again and again. White children rode to school on buses while black children walked long distances on muddy unpaved roads; black graduate and law students seeking admission to segregated universities were seated in a roped-off section outside the classroom or hidden away in a basement office building.[4] In cases involving segregated primary and secondary schools, the inequalities between black and white schools were stark and glaring.

Shortly before Warren was nominated to become chief justice, the Court ruled in favor of two plaintiffs complaining of the unequal conditions they had been forced to endure at segregated institutions. In *Sweatt v. Painter*, the basement "classroom" offered in lieu of a legal education at the University of Texas was found to be a violation of equal protection, and the Court ordered Texas to admit Heman Sweatt "without delay."[5] Similarly, in *McLaurin v. Oklahoma State Regents*, the Court found the segregated education offered by the state to be in no way equal to what the white students at the university were getting. Here, too, the Court ordered the plaintiff admitted.[6] In these pre-*Brown* cases, though, the Court accepted the reality of segregated schooling in an important way: each of these cases focused on the inequality of the conditions under which black and white students were studying. The state had not provided Sweatt or McLaurin an equal education as compared to white students, and that was the basis on which the Court ordered relief. This limited conception of equality did not challenge the ability of state governments to pass and enforce laws that segregated people, in schools and other public spaces, by racial classification.

The rule that "separate but equal" facilities were constitutionally permissible originated in the 1896 precedent of *Plessy v. Ferguson.*[7] In *Plessy*, the plaintiff challenged a Louisiana law that required segregation in railway cars, and in response the Supreme Court ruled that segregation by itself did not deprive Plessy of equal protection of the laws. Thus, the *Plessy* ruling provided legal authority for state-enforced segregation for more than half a century.

Peter Irons has pointed out that the *Plessy* ruling drew its support principally from a pre–Civil War state law case. *Roberts v. Boston*, which was decided by a state court in 1850, declared that the legislature was entitled to make reasonable classifications (including racial ones) in providing public education, and that courts generally could not disturb those classifications.[8] This precedent was hardly authoritative: it was decided by a state court, before the Civil War, and before the Fourteenth Amendment's Equal Protection Clause existed. Besides revealing the shaky ground on which *Plessy* stood, this reliance on a forty-six-year-old state court case indicates the freedom with which the 1890s Supreme Court drew on diverse sources to create federal common law—even when deciding a case that directly raised a substantive constitutional question. Common law, in this view, was certainly something the court could discover by casting about widely and even looking to cases unrelated to the Fourteenth Amendment.

Notwithstanding the questionable provenance of the *Plessy* decision, it stood for fifty-eight years. The Warren Court took the decisive step of overturning *Plessy* (though, to be precise, the Court did not overturn it but simply said it was inapplicable to public education) in a unanimous decision in 1954. Chief Justice Warren rightly predicted the anger and defiance that would follow the decision, and so he acted strategically in writing and issuing it. He secured the support of every justice, including those who had been unwilling, previously, to disturb the "separate but equal" rule. Warren knew that anything less than a unanimous decision would be disastrous because it would signal to the public that not even the Court itself fully supported the major change in social relations catalyzed by the *Brown* ruling. The Court drew on several sources of support for its ruling. First there was the empirical evidence produced through the trial testimony of expert witnesses. Psychologists Kenneth and Mamie Clark of Columbia University had related, at trial, the results of their studies involving children in segregated and nonsegregated schools. When presented with "black" and "white" dolls, students from segregated schools were far more likely to identify and describe the "black" dolls negatively. The Court cited the Clarks' findings, and those of other social scientists, to show that segregation harmed the self-image of African American schoolchildren. In connection with this evidence, the Court emphasized that public schools were a particularly inappropriate setting for racial segregation (here, they were distinguishing *Plessy*, which involved railway transportation rather than education). The weight given to the doll studies reflects the effect of Legal Realism on jurisprudence. Just as the "Brandeis brief" in *Muller v. Oregon* brought social science data to the decisional process earlier, so did the Warren court rely strongly on research psychologists' findings in moving equal protection law forward in *Brown*.

The Court also cited changed social conditions to justify its decision to outlaw segregation in schools. The reader must bear in mind, at this juncture, that the Court faced the tricky institutional problem of saying it had been wrong in the past without discrediting itself overtly. Segregation had been wrong in 1896—that is why Homer Plessy brought his suit. And for that matter, it had been wrong in 1849 when Roberts sued on behalf of his daughter. By citing "changed conditions" and saying "we cannot turn the clock back," the Court glossed over its earlier failing with a minimal loss of institutional legitimacy. This key passage from the *Brown* opinion reads as follows:

> In approaching this problem, we cannot turn the clock back to 1868, when the Amendment was adopted, or even to 1896, when *Plessy v. Ferguson* was written. We must consider public education in the light of its full development and its present place in American life throughout the Nation. Only in this way can it be determined if segregation in public schools deprives these plaintiffs of the equal protection of the laws.[9]

The opinion also notes the changes in public education that had taken place between 1896 and 1954. The public education system had developed so that state-funded schooling was more widespread and consequently formed a larger part of the social experience of the nation's children. Noting this history was another way of leaving *Plessy* behind without confronting the flaws of the decision itself.

Purcell points out that in proclaiming the supremacy of the federal judiciary in interpreting the Constitution, the Court says that "every state legislator and executive and judicial officer is solemnly committed by oath . . . 'to support this Constitution.'" Purcell explains that "By 'this Constitution' the Court emphatically meant the Constitution that it, and it alone, expounded. *Brown* heralded not only new social values and constitutional doctrines but also a new institutional dynamism. It committed the federal judiciary to eliminate legalized racial segregation, and it led the Court to proclaim itself the ultimate voice of the Constitution."[10] What followed after the announcement of the *Brown* decision in 1954 is well known: defiance in words and deeds by state officials in the South, massive resistance to implementing desegregation, threats and intimidation of African American schoolchildren, violent protests, and lethal attacks on black Americans. The Court remained unified, through the Warren years, in its stance against segregation, and several phases of resistance (outright defiance, school closings, and "pupil assignment" practices) were in turn put to rest. Nonetheless, Irons shows that by the start of the twenty-first century, America's public schools were in fact *more* segregated than they had been in 1954—not by law but as a matter of demographic fact (this is known as "de facto segregation," in lawyerly terms). As Irons effectively demonstrates, this phenomenon is the result of a combination of factors: the Court's initial formula of "all deliberate speed," which invited delay in implementing desegregation; the Court's wavering commitment to desegregation over the years as its personnel changed; residential segregation that was often aided by discrimination in the housing market; and insidious and institutionalized racial bias in many areas of social life.

In view of this historical record, many commentators emphasize the failure of the *Brown* decision to eliminate segregation in American life. They suggest that it is unrealistic to uncritically celebrate the decision when racial divisions still loom so large sixty years later. But between these poles—celebration on the one hand and denial of its importance on the other—there is a middle ground that has relevance for this study of common law constitutionalism. The Warren court's *Brown* opinion catalyzed social change in numerous ways. It gave force to the civil rights movement. It removed legal barriers to equality that had stood for 300 years. It provided educational opportunities for many students who then went on to prominence in law, politics, and academia. It led to the passage of the 1964 Civil Rights Act. All of this is well known. But, in addition, the Court took up what Rogers Smith has called a challenge to liberalism by seeking to give meaning to equality and inclusion in American social life.[11] The Court acted when Congress was unwilling to do so, and it brought criticism on itself from virtually every corner of public life. It sought to take the unwritten law of human equality and weld it to the written constitution. In this sense, the Warren Court's decision in *Brown* furthered the tradition of common law constitutionalism in a fundamental and important way.

This equality jurisprudence has been called "substantive equal protection"[12]—a term that emphasizes the Court's expansion of "equal protection" in the same way that "substantive due process" expands the notion of due process. To be sure, there is potential for conflict between the values of "liberty" (promoted by due process) and "equality" (promoted by equal protection). At the end of this chapter, I will have more to say about the relationship between liberty and equality in constitutional law. For now, it suffices to say that the Warren Court's impact on constitutionalism through its equal protection jurisprudence is a powerful legacy that stands alongside the more readily observable changes wrought by *Brown v. Board of Education*.

Incorporation of the Bill of Rights against the States

"Incorporation" is the term used to describe the process by which the Warren Court applied the specific guarantees of the Constitution's first ten amendments—that is, the Bill of Rights—against the states. Central to the incorporation process is the phrase "due process of law," whose roots lie, as we have seen, in the "law of the land" provision of the Magna Carta's Article 39. Due process refers generally to limits on the government's power to act against individuals. Such actions must be authorized by law: they must follow the law in procedure and substance. By incorporating the Bill of Rights, the Court was able to limit the power of the states to act against individuals in the context of criminal proceedings and in other contexts.

The phrase "due process of law" appears in the Fifth Amendment, but it is repeated in the Fourteenth Amendment, which was adopted just after the Civil War. A review of the language of the Bill of Rights confirms that its provisions were included in the Constitution in the first place as a safeguard against federal power. "*Congress* shall make no law," the First Amendment begins, and then it goes on to list freedoms of religion, speech, press, assembly, and petition that are protected against federal government infringement. During the ratification period, the Anti-Federalists feared that a central, federal government would overreach its powers and oppress the people as well as the individual states. The limiting guarantees of the Bill of Rights represented an enforceable assurance that such overreaching would not be permitted. The substantive guarantees contained in the Bill of Rights were functionally related to "due process" because they marked out limits for government behavior. For instance, when seeking to deprive a person of liberty via criminal trial, conviction, and sentence, the government could not coerce a confession, could not impose cruel and unusual punishment, and could not deny the opportunity to confront witnesses. "Due process of law" required the federal government to observe those limits.

Nearly a century later, in a very different political climate, the Constitution was amended once again to insert another due process guarantee. This time, it was a guarantee that the *states* would observe the limits of law in their actions against individuals. This much is clear enough, but it leads to an obvious and unavoidable question: What is the *meaning* of "due process" in this more recent addition to the constitutional text? Should rules of criminal procedure, for example, generated from the Bill of Rights apply only in prosecutions by the federal government, or should they apply in state court prosecutions as well?

Generally, and one by one, the Warren Court did incorporate the Bill of Rights into the due process guarantee of the Fourteenth Amendment. Here, by way of example, are some of the best-known Warren court incorporation cases in the criminal law context:

- *Mapp v. Ohio* (1964).[13] *Mapp* applied the Fourth Amendment's exclusionary rule to state court prosecutions. This means that evidence seized in an "unreasonable search" cannot be used as evidence in a state court criminal prosecution against the person searched. Prior to *Mapp*, the exclusionary rule was applied in federal but not state criminal prosecutions. The rule was intended to deter police misconduct in the form of warrantless searches.

- *Miranda v. Arizona* (1966).[14] *Miranda* incorporated the Fifth Amendment's self-incrimination clause against the states. Specifically, *Miranda* required that criminal suspects be read a statement of their right not to speak to law enforcement authorities and also directed law enforcement to cease questioning immediately any suspect who indicated a desire not to speak. The *Miranda* requirement was intended to guard against involuntary (coerced) confessions.
- *Gideon v. Wainwright* (1963).[15] This case involved the Sixth Amendment's "right to counsel" clause. Gideon was charged with burglary but was unable to afford legal counsel. The trial judge denied Gideon's request for state-funded legal representation because under Florida law only capital (death penalty) defendants were entitled to counsel at the state's expense. The Court ruled in Gideon's favor, applying the Sixth Amendment to the states and announcing the right to counsel in noncapital cases.

These rulings produced major changes in state law enforcement as well as federal-state relations. They increased the role of the federal courts in overseeing the criminal justice process and increased the amount of appellate litigation.

The incorporation of the Bill of Rights via Fourteenth Amendment due process could be explained and defended in different two ways. An "originalist" argument would rely on evidence of what the drafters of the Constitution intended the relevant terms to mean, or what those terms meant to Americans at the time. Hugo Black derived his incorporation theory in this way, using evidence of the framers' intent as support for the incorporation of the Bill of Rights provisions. In the 1947 case of *Adamson v. California*, Black wrote, "I would follow what I believe was the original purpose of the Fourteenth Amendment to extend to all the people of the nation the complete protection of the Bill of Rights."[16] Black was a liberal justice in the sense that he favored the use of judicial power to aid vulnerable groups, including criminal defendants. But his interpretive approach was to look to the intentions of the framers in order to discern the meaning of specific constitutional provisions.

Justice Frankfurter advocated incorporation from a different perspective. Frankfurter's judicial philosophy was somewhat complex. He was a Progressive who believed in the legislature's ability to address social problems, and he was a strong supporter of the New Deal. This led him to defer, at times, to legislative judgments. But he also believed that judges had the special ability—and responsibility—to resolve legal conflicts with an eye to all of their dimensions, including political context and the equities involved. Thus he could support the desegregation mandate of *Brown* while voting a decade earlier to uphold the internment of Japanese Americans on the West Coast. It is his faith in judicial reason that helps to explain Frankfurter's expansive conception of due process. He saw due process in much the same way that earlier common law judges did, even as it was applied in the modern context to incorporate the Bill of Rights. Here is Frankfurter expounding on due process in the 1949 case of *Wolf v. Colorado*:

> "Due process of law" conveys neither formal nor fixed nor narrow requirements. It is the compendious expression for all those rights which the courts must enforce because they are basic to our free society. But basic rights do not become petrified as of any one time, even though, as a matter of

> human experience, some may not too rhetorically be called eternal verities. It is of the very nature of a free society to advance its standards of what is deemed reasonable and right. Representing as it does a living principle, due process is not confined within a permanent catalogue of what may at a given time be deemed the limits or essentials of fundamental rights.[17]

Wolf was a Fourth Amendment search and seizure case later overruled by *Mapp v. Ohio*, which is described above. For present purposes, *Wolf* is significant because Frankfurter's opinion there finds the Due Process Clause to protect fundamental rights against state intrusion. In 1949, the Court was not prepared to apply the exclusionary rule against the states (that would come later, in *Mapp*), but Frankfurter did reveal a conception of due process as "compendious," and protective of rights that are "basic to our free society." He differed from Black in the way he reached the conclusion that incorporation was warranted. Black looked for evidence indicating that the drafters meant for the Bill of Rights to apply against the states, while Frankfurter focused on the meaning of due process, which he construed in broader and more flexible terms. Frankfurter's more capacious notion of due process is consistent with the Magna Carta tradition. As we have seen, judges and commentators in England and the United States cited the "law of the land" provision of Article 39 of the Magna Carta as a guarantee of fundamental liberty, and Justice Curtis in the mid-nineteenth century showed how "due process" replaced "law of the land" to guarantee fundamental liberty in the U.S. Constitution. Frankfurter's exposition of "due process" tracks the earlier ones fairly closely. The guarantee is ancient and powerful yet open to developing interpretations and flexible application.

Griswold v. Connecticut: *Privacy as Due Process*

Griswold is an extremely important case in the history of the Due Process Clause. It not only applies the Bill of Rights (via the Fourteenth Amendment Due Process Clause) to strike down a state law but also construes several constitutional provisions, in combination, to form a new kind of privacy guarantee. The case involved a state criminal law prohibiting use of contraception, even by married couples, and also prohibited physicians from counseling patients regarding contraception. Justice Douglas wrote an opinion for the Court in which he articulated a privacy right formed from implicit privacy references in the Bill of Rights. This was a form of "substantive due process" that was seen previously in *Lochner v. New York*, but the newer form of substantive due process seen in *Griswold* applied not to economic rights but rather to privacy in intimate relations. In fact, at the start of his opinion, Douglas explicitly disavowed any reliance on *Lochner*.[18] Over the course of the twentieth century, *Lochner* had fallen into disrepute.

After distancing himself from *Lochner*, Douglas went on to explain how he derived implicit privacy rights from the constitutional text. The problem he faced was that the explicit reference to privacy in the Bill of Rights is found in the Fourth Amendment, which refers to law enforcement–related searches. But Douglas wanted to construe privacy more broadly than as a criminal procedural right. He cited several cases involving privacy concerns outside of the search and seizure context and then added, "The foregoing cases suggest that specific guarantees in the Bill of Rights have penumbras, formed by emanations from those guarantees that help give them life and substance."[19] The concept of a "penumbra" allowed Douglas to speak of "zones" of privacy related to but not mentioned in the text of the Constitution. He continued: "The present case, then, concerns a relationship lying within the zone of privacy created by several fundamental constitutional guarantees. And it concerns a law which, in forbidding the use of contraceptives, rather than regulating their manufacture or sale, seeks to achieve its goals by means having a maximum destructive impact upon that relationship."[20] This decision voided a retrograde and ill-advised state law. Douglas's "zones of privacy" language also laid the foundation for other substantive due process cases involving privacy, including *Roe v. Wade* (1973), which extended the right to privacy so that it protected a woman's right to terminate pregnancy.[21] *Griswold* also helped to generate *Lawrence v. Texas* (2003), which extended the right to privacy again to protect same-sex intimate relationships from state intrusion.[22]

The *Griswold* decision is consistent with common law constitutionalism—and Douglas was, in an important sense, "a common-law judge on the nation's highest court," as Melvin Urofsky has described him.[23] Urofsky explained, "By this view, it is the obligation of the judge to face policy issues squarely, to read moral norms into the law, even if at times discerning what those norms are is a difficult task. In short it is the duty of the common law courts as it is of the legislative branches to make law."[24] This comment shows how far common law constitutionalism has moved, by the 1960s, from its more conservative orientation in the late nineteenth and earlier twentieth centuries. It is no longer oriented toward protecting economic elites but rather toward the individual liberty of Americans generally. The shared link is that the federal courts functioned powerfully in shaping constitutional doctrine in both eras. But the legacy of Legal Realism can be seen in the later era, and in fact Douglas himself was involved in the Realist movement when he taught at Yale.[25] So the strong and vital role that Douglas saw for the federal courts in constitutional development bore the imprint of decades of Realist scholarship and commentary. The Realist judges were, of course, more forthright than their predecessors had been about their consideration of outside factors in rendering decisions. And in a sense, Douglas's embrace of Realism provided a defense against critics who faulted his willingness to evade doctrinal limitations. Douglas saw his role as a justice (or, in Urofsky's terms, as a common law judge) as requiring him to protect fundamental liberties against state interference even if doctrine itself stood as an obstacle to getting there. Thus, as Urofsky points out, this was a virtue in the eyes of many just as it was a vice in the eyes of Douglas's critics—and what is more, Douglas can be seen in retrospect to have "gotten it right" in the sense that his antidoctrine has now become doctrine.[26] "By asking the right questions, by engaging in unorthodox analysis," he says, Douglas "got it right far more often" as compared with Frankfurter, whose opinions were usually viewed as more scholarly and truer to the constitutional text.[27] Douglas was influential as he sat on the Court during (and six years beyond) the Warren era as it sought "to be responsive to the needs of a changing society," and his influence "helped keep that common-law tradition [of flexibility and capacity for growth and adaptation] alive."[28]

Habeas Corpus in Fay v. Noia

The growth of the constitutional rights of criminal defendants during the Warren years extended even to cases that did not directly implicate the Bill of Rights. *Fay v. Noia* (1963)[29] gave the Court another opportunity to strengthen the rights of criminal defendants, but this time in connection with habeas corpus rights. The Court's ruling broadened the availability of habeas corpus relief in proceedings arising out of state court prosecutions. In *Fay*, three defendants had been convicted for their roles in a robbery/homicide, but two of them were later freed after showing that their confessions had been coerced. The third defendant,

Noia, sought relief from conviction on the same grounds, but the lower court ruled that his failure to appeal the conviction in the past barred a subsequent habeas corpus petition. Justice Brennan wrote a majority opinion holding that Noia could seek relief via habeas corpus despite his failure to appeal. In reaching this result, Brennan had to address federalism concerns. Shouldn't the state law procedural default be considered in construing the federal remedy? And didn't federal courts defer to states in such instances as a matter of comity? Brennan answered both of these questions in the negative. "The jurisdiction of federal courts on habeas corpus," he wrote, "is not affected by procedural defaults by the applicant during state court proceedings."[30] And comity had to be distinguished from power in the sense that the federal courts had the power to do what comity sometimes moved them to refrain from doing. In this case, comity considerations had to give way to the demands of justice.[31]

Brennan traced the origins of habeas corpus back through English history, making explicit reference to the Magna Carta. In doing so, he linked habeas corpus to the "law of the land" phraseology of the Magna Carta. Referencing a 1593 bill that was never enacted, he said, "The bill accurately prefigured the union of the right to due process drawn from Magna Charta and the remedy of habeas corpus accomplished in the next century [by the Habeas Corpus Act]."[32] Connecting due process and habeas corpus to a common source in the Magna Carta is important in the development of common law constitutionalism because the "law of the land" reference in Article 39 can then be seen to generate support for habeas corpus as a remedy at the same time that it imposes procedural standards on state detention. As Brennan puts it, "It is of the historical essence of habeas corpus that it lies to test proceedings so fundamentally lawless that imprisonment pursuant to them is not merely erroneous but void."[33]

Speaking of the "historical essence" of habeas corpus in this way evokes a sense that meanings of legal concepts develop over time and by means of tradition. The lineage and history of habeas corpus shape its meaning, for Brennan, in 1963: "At the time the privilege of the writ was written into the Federal Constitution it was settled that the writ lay to test any restraint contrary to fundamental law, which in England stemmed from Magna Charta but in this country was embodied in the written constitution."[34] He made it clear that the linkage of habeas corpus to the Magna Carta was significant in construing the meaning of habeas corpus, but he also emphasized the *embodied*, written law source of habeas corpus in U.S. law. In part, this is merely lawyerly argumentation on Brennan's part: fixing one's position in the most secure and indisputable authority of written law makes the argument stronger. At the same time, though, he does mention the Magna Carta in the same sentence, which allows him to draw on English tradition to flesh out the meaning of liberty in this particular sense. Here in *Noia*, a mid-twentieth-century U.S. criminal case, Brennan cites earlier commentary and famous English trials in support of the Court's ability to do justice consistent with what written law provides—and, in the sense that the ruling sets aside state law, *despite* what written law provides. Habeas corpus is "predestined by its historical role"; it is "one of the precious heritages of Anglo-American civilization."[35]

Voting Rights

Voting rights was another area in which the Warren court made important—and controversial—case law that tended to protect and expand individual rights. Some of these cases were tied to race discrimination, and some were not. Although the Fifteenth Amendment addresses voting rights specifically, the Court often drew on the concept of equal protection in the course of reaching a decision. Here are several representative and important voting rights decisions:

- *Baker v. Carr* (1962).[36] This case challenged Tennessee's apportionment of voting districts for which members of the House of Representatives would be elected. The apportionment scheme had been in effect unchanged since 1901, and it had the effect of diluting the voting strength of African American voters. Plaintiffs here sought an order directing the state to reapportion the districts in light of changed demographics over the course of sixty years. Rejecting the argument that this was a "political question" in which the courts could not interfere, Justice Brennan's majority opinion ruled that the Equal protection Clause required reapportionment.
- *Harper v. West Virginia* (1966).[37] This case invalidated a state law requiring payment of a poll tax in order to vote. Citing the fundamental importance of the right to vote, the Court proclaimed that that right could not be conditioned in any way upon the ability to pay for it. Moreover, the majority opinion by Justice Douglas affirmed the Court's intention to read "equal protection" in an expansive way that could connect with long-standing tradition and supersede historical context: "The Equal Protection Clause is not shackled to the political theory of a particular era. In determining what lines are unconstitutionally discriminatory, we have never been confined to historic notions of equality, any more than we have restricted due process to a fixed catalogue of what was at a given time deemed to be the limits of fundamental rights."[38] In this interesting and important passage, Douglas provides a concise description of the interplay of common law constitutionalism's simultaneous orientation to the past and the future. The conceptions of due process and equal protection were not fixed or static—they could be adapted as new contexts and conflicts arose (this aspect looks to the future). But their enduring importance was shown by the

very fact that were claimed and applied, time and again, in successive eras (this aspect looks to the past). What tied them together with earlier conceptions was the body of decisional law generated by judges—that is, common law constitutionalism.

- *Katzenbach v. Morgan* (1966).[39] New York election law required voters to be able to read and write in English in order to vote. This law conflicted with Section 4(e) of the Voting Rights Act of 1965, which applied specifically to schools in Puerto Rico and allowed students who had attended those schools (through sixth grade) the right to vote. The plaintiffs sought enforcement of the New York English-language law (barring non–English speakers from voting) despite Section 4(e) of the federal law. The Court had to decide the scope of enforcement power under the Fourteenth Amendment: Did it authorize Section 4(e) as "appropriate" equal protection enforcement legislation? The Court held that it did, and the practical result was that Puerto Rican voters could vote even if they did not meet the English-language test under state law.

Criticisms

It is to be expected that a thoroughgoing revolution in legal thought and decisional law such as the Warren Court accomplished would be met with criticism from the legal establishment as well as from sectors of the American public. To be sure, there were groups who felt threatened by the changes brought by the Court's involvement in deeply rooted disputes such as the struggle over segregation. And the Court certainly did face attacks from multiple directions. The anticommunist movement attacked the justices for their rulings on speech and associational freedoms, and the states' rights Southerners and segregationists criticized them viciously as well for striking down Jim Crow laws.[40] Arkansas governor Orval Faubus (among many others) openly defied the Court's desegregation mandate in his state, to the point where President Eisenhower had to send federal troops to enforce it. This background of public opposition is important to remember in assessing the Court's efforts "to be responsive to the needs of a changing society," as Urofsky puts it. It is much more difficult to insist on the requirements of justice when support outside the judiciary is inconsistent at best and nonexistent at worst.[41]

Criticisms came from within the academic community as well. Some commentators, such as future chief justice William Rehnquist, were opposed to overturning *Plessy* and therefore disagreed with the end result in that case as well as the means employed to get there. Others—such as Alexander Bickel and Henry Hart—were sympathetic to the cause of racial justice but took issue with the Court's methodology. Bickel, who had been a law clerk and protégé of Frankfurter's, wrote an important book at the close of the Warren era in which he faulted the Court for "imagin[ing] the past and remember[ing] the future," and getting both of them wrong.[42] Regarding the past, Bickel thought that the Warren Court had "imagined" it in a way that conflicted with the evidence. "On more than a few occasions," Bickel wrote, "the Warren Court has purported to discover in the history of the Fourteenth Amendment, and of the Thirteenth, and of other constitutional provisions, the crutch that wasn't there."[43] This flawed historical inquiry, he suggested, helped the Court to spin a "web of subjectivity,"[44] so that one flaw led to another to form a structure that was interdependent upon weak components. Thus, with this critique Bickel could put into question most of the Warren Court's jurisprudence.

With regard to the future, Bickel accused the Court of "misremembering"—or misperceiving—the direction of progress. He distinguished between the "old" and "new" constitutional faiths and their different ideas of progress. The nineteenth-century and early twentieth-century Supreme Court had an idea of progress that aligned with industrial development and the interests of economic elites. The justices were conservative in the sense that they rebuffed challenges to the dominance of business interests (as in *Lochner*, for example), but they saw their role as helping economic elites move society forward through the discovery of objectively correct and true principles of jurisprudence. The "new" constitutional faith of Progressivism, by contrast, led later Courts to defer to the legislature—to "allow" rather than lead progress.[45] The changing social conditions of the 1950s and 1960s, which the Warren Court both responded to and helped to bring about, posed a challenge to the "new" faith, Bickel thought, because once progress was in the hands of (human) judges, it became crucial for those judges to identify the direction of progress correctly.[46] Bickel thought the Warren Court had erred by not foreseeing the course of the desegregation and voting conflicts in their full and complex development over the next two decades—an accurate, if unrealistic, criticism.

Bickel faulted the Court, above all, for being unprincipled. As he put it, "The Court is the place for principled judgment disciplined by the method of reason familiar to the discourse of moral philosophy, and in constitutional adjudication, the place for only that, or else its insulation from the political process is inexplicable."[47] In this passage Bickel uses the terms "principled judgment" and "reason" in a narrow sense. Principles guided the jurisprudence of the Warren Court, but they were principles in broad outline, such as the promotion of social and political equality. And "reason" can be paired with a variety of adjectives to describe aspects of the judicial role. Not only the practice of applying abstract logic but also the fashioning of pragmatic decisional law are forms of judicial reason. His reference to moral philosophy, too, needs further explanation. Douglas's conception of privacy, for example, relies on a moral foundation even if it is not the same one Bickel would invoke. Ronald Dworkin would defend Bill of Rights jurisprudence from his particular version of natural law. It is one thing to take issue with the Warren Court's principles, and quite another to say that *no* principles are evident in the Court's decisions.

Bickel thought that there had been "countless lapses" in the use of reason and principle over the history of Supreme Court decision making.[48] Somehow, though, the Warren Court was an outlier in his view, and worse than the rest, because earlier courts that erred "never put in question the value of rigorous analysis."[49]

What are we to make of Bickel's criticism of the Warren Court? It is true that the Court took a freer approach to construing precedent than its immediate predecessors, and it is certainly true as well that it was mindful of the historical context in which its cases arose. Three of the Warren Court's most influential justices over its sixteen-year life span—Warren, Douglas, and Brennan—favored decision-making methodologies that emphasized those concerns. Warren came to the Court and set out immediately to engineer a consensus to end state-enforced racial segregation. Douglas was a "common law judge" who sought to broaden individual liberty through case law, as his *Griswold* opinion exemplifies. Brennan shared his colleagues' commitments to liberty and equality, and he pursued those commitments in a pragmatic way. Of the three, Brennan was the most willing to explain publicly his approach to constitutional law—as, for example, in his article on the Bill of Rights where he envisioned a "dialogue" between legislature and court over rights principles. Each branch could correct the other, and through the process a workable and enduring set of parameters for individual rights could be achieved.[50] Bickel acknowledged that there had been "countless lapses" from "principled judgment" in the Court's history before the 1950s; it is possible that the ones he perceived in the Warren years were worse than earlier ones, for him, because of the controversy they stirred. But it was not controversy for its own sake; rather, the Court acted to protect rights (I am speaking particularly of the desegregation and voting rights cases here) when the other branches were unwilling to do so. Bickel himself concedes that in the Warren era democracy was not functioning for black Americans in the Jim Crow South.[51]

Bickel was a student and protégé of Frankfurter, and their relationship helps to explain the shape and focus of Bickel's criticism of the Warren Court. Frankfurter escapes criticism entirely in the book, and in fact Bickel often *sounds* like Frankfurter when he faults the Court for deficiencies of principle and reason. As Urofsky points out, Frankfurter was known as the scholar on the Warren Court, but he had little lasting influence on the Court in terms of its legacy or the development of constitutional law.[52] It is quite plausible to read *The Supreme Court and the Idea of Progress* as Bickel's attempt to defend his mentor. Also, Frankfurter had deputized Bickel to research the history of the Fourteenth Amendment as to education and the existence of segregation during the drafting and ratification process. Bickel published his results in the *Harvard Law Review* years before. Thus, it is not surprising that he is particularly concerned with the Court's reading of history, as that was a major focus of Bickel's scholarly work. Amar acknowledges that racial segregation was the norm in 1868, but he nonetheless argues that the intent of the Fourteenth Amendment was to establish equality.[53] Amar reads the history to be more complex.

Henry Hart was another prominent legal scholar who criticized the Warren Court for its method while supporting some of its accomplishments. He supported the result in *Brown v. Board of Education*, but like Bickel he thought the Court was wrong in the way it approached precedent and developed new doctrine. Hart had undertaken the long-term study of federal jurisprudence, and in that process he came to focus on a system-level understanding of the federal courts and to appreciate the importance of federalism concerns. Also, his long involvement in the federal government led him to incorporate certain policy outlooks in his own legal thought: particularly, the need to protect government from subversive influences, and the need to preserve the institutional innovations of the New Deal.[54] What emerged from this mix of influences was a jurisprudence that emphasized process, and, as Purcell notes, "The idea of law as process fit nicely with Hart's conviction that law should be based on principles."[55] While it is true that Hart's process approach tended to "minimize[e] social conflict and economic inequality,"[56] he also believed that the federal courts were uniquely capable of providing a "juster justice" to litigants.[57] Like Bickel, Hart attacked the Warren Court for flaws in reasoning and lack of principle. And yet, as Purcell notes perceptively, Hart unintentionally lent support and defense to the Warren Court's accomplishments by virtue of his own view of the role of the federal courts in providing "juster justice." "The Warren court confounded him," Purcell suggested, "because it embodied, albeit in a form he found unsatisfactory, many of his fundamental values and ideals: judicial creativity, protection of individual liberty, institutional recognition of moral principles, the lawmaking primacy of the federal courts, the inspiring effort to establish a 'juster justice,' and a deep belief in the cause of racial justice itself."[58]

Experience has proved the Warren Court correct on a number of points. *Brown* is widely regarded as the correct decision today, no matter where a commentator sits on the liberal-conservative spectrum. State-enforced racial segregation is a practice that no serious scholar or policy maker would advocate today. Incorporation of the Bill of Rights has become a familiar aspect of criminal procedure. When the Roberts Court struck down a portion of the Voting Rights Act in 2013, its decision was met by shock and anger. In short, one measure of the correctness of the Court's choice of principles in the 1950s and 1960s is the way its decisions have become part of the constitutional ethos in the ensuing half century. In support of his charge that Warren "remembered the future" incorrectly, Bickel posits a rather fanciful hypothetical case where racial discrimination is not associated with socioeconomic disadvantage, where separation by race takes place without an unequal distribution of resources. In such a case, he suggests, segregation by socioeconomic status would be more harmful than segregation by race. Evidently Bickel was suggesting that level of wealth rather than race would have been a more effective basis for developing inclusive educational opportunity.[59] But this is idle speculation about a society that did not exist, and it could provide no useful answers in connection with the actually existing social relations confronting the Supreme Court at midcentury.

Conclusion

Broadly speaking, the work of the Warren Court can be subsumed under the themes of liberty and equality (which correspond, of course, to due process and equal protection). Due process has a direct semantic connection to the Magna Carta's Article 39. As for equality, the legal meaning of that concept expanded greatly in the 1950s and 1960s. It was often twinned with due process in order to make reference to basic and ancient rights (as Justice Douglas referenced them in *Harper*). In one sense equality and liberty are at odds: the former views the social body as an undifferentiated group, while the latter emphasizes individuality. But it is also possible to connect the two concepts as facets of fair treatment. The individual wishes to be treated according to law when the government acts against her (due process). At the same time, she does not want to be singled out, as an individual or group, for differential treatment (equal protection). Both of these facets of fairness are fundamental to the rule of law.

The methodology used by Warren Court justices to pursue those ends is consistent with common law constitutionalism.

In describing Douglas as a common law judge, Urofsky pinpoints one aspect of that legacy: the creation of precedent that responded to urgent concerns and stood the test of later applications. Subsequent experience has shown that Douglas "asked the right questions and got the right answers." The form of reason he applied to problems of privacy and other aspects of liberty was not the reasoning of the syllogism, but rather a more supple form of reason. Drawing on tradition, and sometimes deviating from it, he sought to elaborate a normative basis for protecting individuality in modern society. He was guided by the conceptions of liberty and equality that he set forth in *Harper*: not dependent on historical context but nonetheless capable of adaptation and development. Placed alongside the work of other proponents of common law constitutionalism from earlier periods, Douglas's opinions fit well.

Similarly, Justice Brennan's written work, both in court opinions and in extraneous commentary, exemplifies aspects of common law constitutionalism. Brennan was pragmatic and flexible in his thinking. He viewed the Constitution as a living document that was written in open terms in order to adapt to changing conditions. And yet, for Brennan, the protection of human liberty and dignity was a basic and constant duty of judges. This duty could be discharged through constant awareness of the traditions of liberty stretching back to the Magna Carta, and Brennan was explicit about this.

Thus, the Warren Court's influential personnel, and its body of decisions, can be seen as consistent with common law constitutionalism as previously practiced. But how well did the continuation of common law constitutionalism serve the nation at that point (1950s–1960s) in its development? Here, we can turn again to Bickel. He asks a rhetorical question about the Warren Court and the future. After laying out, one more time, his charges of methodological error against the Court, he says, "It is nevertheless clear what the Court has identified as the general direction of progress, where its sympathies and preferences lie, and is that not good enough?"[60] As I have said, the case law of the Warren era has held up quite well over a half century. Amar notes that in contemporary debates, both liberals and conservatives claim for themselves the "true" legacy of *Brown* and the voting rights decisions.[61] These widespread endorsements are indeed "good enough" to vindicate the Court's estimation of the direction of progress; such consensus has proved helpful, if not sufficient, in pursuing justice.

Channeling Frankfurter, Bickel also makes reference to the "conversation" between the legislature and the Court—through this two-way process, responsible and enduring law is made.[62] As I have noted, Justice Brennan made a similar point about a dialogical interbranch relationship. I think that it is possible to acknowledge that such dialogue is necessary and productive and also to depict it within the Warren Court's desegregation cases. A conversation between legislature and Court was needed in the 1940s and 1950s, but it was not happening. *Brown* can be seen as the *initiation* of that conversation, which continued with the passage of civil rights laws and other legislative enactments. Without its 1954 ruling, that particular conversation would have taken a lot longer to get started.

6

The Rehnquist Court and Habeas Corpus Retrenchment

> There is no basis in text, tradition, or even in contemporary practice (if that were enough), for finding in the Constitution a right to demand judicial consideration of newly discovered evidence of innocence brought forward after conviction.
>
> Justice Scalia, concurring in *Herrera v. Collins*

> The execution of a person who can show that he is innocent comes perilously close to simple murder.
>
> Justice Blackmun, dissenting in *Herrera v. Collins*

Habeas corpus, the topic of this chapter, has been discussed at other points in this book. It is the form of legal proceeding by which a state custodian of a prisoner is ordered to physically produce the prisoner's body in court. The order to "bring forth the body" is triggered by a petition stating that the prisoner's detention violates fundamental law. If successful, a habeas corpus action leads to the prisoner's release from custody.

Although habeas corpus predates the Magna Carta, we have seen that the two of them—the Great Charter and the Great Writ—are often mentioned together. This is because Article 39's prohibition on detention except by "law of the land" eventually came to be enforced through the writ of habeas corpus. Article

39's "law of the land" clause has generated two strands of doctrine related to individual liberty: due process of law and habeas corpus. These two doctrines intertwine to some extent as both are employed to require lawful actions by a detaining authority, but they are distinct in the sense that habeas corpus is a specific form of legal proceeding whereas due process is a flexible set of standards. To be precise, habeas corpus is a form of collateral challenge to detention. It is different from a direct appeal, which attacks the prisoner's conviction by asking a higher court to review it. Habeas corpus is available more widely. It can be used after appeals are exhausted, even by prisoners who have not been charged or convicted at all. This wider availability is what makes habeas corpus such a crucial right, but it also makes habeas cases and procedures a source of controversy, as habeas often frees prisoners who were convicted long before (the boxer Rubin "Hurricane" Carter is a good example). The attempts by the Rehnquist Court (and Congress) to curtail habeas rights, and the opposition to those attempts, are easier to understand when one keeps in mind the historical origins and development of the Great Writ.

The "Law and Order" Perspective of the Rehnquist Court

William Rehnquist became chief justice in 1986, and during the two decades he presided over the Court, there was a pronounced conservative orientation to its decisions. Of course, what one means by "conservative" in the context of judicial decision making must be specified, since the term can be understood in a variety of ways. As David Shapiro noted long ago, Rehnquist's judicial conservatism resulted in three types of case outcomes: he tended to favor states' rights over federal power, government over individual rights, and denial of federal court jurisdiction over granting it.[1] These tendencies are reflected in the decisional law of the 1986–2005 time period, and the Rehnquist Court is known for its conservative "retrenchment"[2] on states' rights, civil liberties, and federal court jurisdiction. While some have argued that the Rehnquist Court was most "revolutionary" in the area of federalism by preferring and protecting states' rights,[3] it cannot be denied that the Court under Rehnquist accomplished a significant curtailment of the rights of criminal defendants. This effect is due in large part to the Court's decisions on habeas corpus during the period. In several important rulings, the Court restricted the availability of habeas corpus for postconviction petitioners: those seeking to show their innocence through newly discovered evidence, those seeking the benefit of retroactive application of a new rule, and those contesting the Antiterrorism and Effective Death Penalty Act (AEDPA) of 1996. With these decisions, the Rehnquist Court responded to and repudiated the pro-defendant orientation of the Warren Court. This was hardly a coincidence. Rehnquist had been nominated as associate justice by a president (Nixon) who emphasized "law and order," and he was elevated to chief justice by another president (Reagan) who sought to define himself as "tough on crime."[4] Early on—before becoming chief—Rehnquist had signaled that he was "impatient" with the Court's deadlock over death penalty issues, and he sought rules changes that would speed up the process of death penalty review.[5] Congress passed the AEDPA at the midpoint of the Rehnquist era, adding momentum to the rightward movement of criminal law that was already under way. In this chapter I will highlight some of the consequential habeas rulings by the Rehnquist Court and show how they functioned as a "course correction" to Warren Court criminal jurisprudence and, in a larger sense, to the habeas corpus component of the Magna Carta tradition.

A "Rule against New Rules" in Habeas Cases: Teague v. Lane *(1989)*

Teague v. Lane[6] was an important Supreme Court decision that limited petitioners' ability to benefit from new decisional law when crafting habeas petitions. Stephen Feldman has termed the *Teague* holding a "rule against new rules." As he explains it, "The Teague rule against new rules prohibits, with two narrow exceptions, federal habeas courts from announcing or applying new rules of constitutional law. Hence, a state prisoner can gain relief only by showing that the state courts ignored or misapplied an old rule of law."[7]

Teague, who was African American, had been convicted, by an all-white jury, of attempted murder and other offenses. The prosecutor had used all ten peremptory challenges[8] to exclude African American jurors from the jury empaneled to try Teague's case. After exhausting his direct appeals, Teague filed a petition for habeas corpus alleging a constitutional violation in the jury selection process. The Supreme Court found Teague's habeas petition to be barred because it would require the creation of a new rule not in effect when his direct appeals ended and his conviction became final. The Court drew a distinction, here, between challenges in the direct appeal process on the one hand and collateral challenges through habeas petitions on the other. Because Teague urged an interpretation of the Sixth Amendment's "impartial jury" provision that they thought amounted to a "new rule," the plurality found that claim to be barred and refused to hear it. But they were aware of the ambiguity inherent in this "rule against new rules" even as they tried to explicate it: "It is admittedly often difficult to determine when a case announces a new rule, and we do not attempt to define the spectrum of what may or may not constitute a new rule for retroactivity purposes. In general, however, a case announces a new rule when it breaks new ground or imposes a new obligation on the States or the Federal Government."[9]

The Court's further discussion only clouded the matter. "To put it differently," it continued, "a case announces a new rule if the result was not *dictated* by precedent existing at the time the defendant's conviction became final."[10] This statement presents significant interpretive difficulties. As the dissent points out, "Few decisions on appeal or collateral review are '*dictated*' by what came before. Most such cases involve a question of law that is at least debatable, permitting a rational judge to resolve the case in more than one way. Virtually no case that prompts a dissent on the relevant legal point, for example, could be said to be '*dictated*' by prior decisions."[11] If the mere presence of a dissenting opinion attached to a case signals that its rule is unsettled, then the universe of "settled" law is small indeed. The "rule against new rules," then, dramatically restricts the claims that can be raised in a petition for habeas corpus and prevents merits review by barring the claim before it can even be considered any time a petitioner seeks to establish a "new rule."

Feldman takes this critique a step further by viewing the problem as one of the general indeterminacy of language. Utilizing insights from postmodern theories of language, he notes that language always negotiates between tradition and innovation. To be intelligible, language requires a community of interpreters who share certain fundamental background assumptions that allow communication to take place. These assumptions can also be described as interpretive traditions. So it is not just judicial opinions but all forms of language that unfold against a background of interpretive tradition.

Yet tradition is only part of the meaning-construction process, for every use of language undermines the partial stability, or fixity, of meaning that existed beforehand. Just as tradition always shapes meaning, new acts of speech (innovation) always *undermine* meaning. This means that each communicative act is neither fully repetitive nor wholly new. Communication takes place within this unstable relationship between tradition and innovation. As Feldman puts it, "The meaning of a legal rule comes into being anew each time we understand, interpret, and apply it. No legal rule exists apart from the social practices that constantly create and recreate it. No matter how deeply a rule appears embedded in our legal tradition, the hermeneutic act of understanding necessarily reconstructs that tradition and consequently reconstitutes the rule."[12]

This is a key insight yielded by postmodernism, and it provides another avenue of critique of the *Teague* rule against new rules.[13] The critique sharpens when Feldman puts Rehnquist himself in the role of postmodern ironist. He notes that Rehnquist's subsequent discussion of the *Teague* rule against new rules plays with the new rule/old rule problematic. Rehnquist suggests that even when a court *thinks* it's applying an old rule, it could be wrong. What looks like a settled rule may not be. Completing this rhetorical turn, Rehnquist acknowledges that his Court, which has the last word, can term a rule old or new, as it pleases. Indeterminacy of meaning serves power by allowing the Court to dismiss habeas petitions by calling them, in effect, new rules disguised as old ones. In words he attributes to the ironist chief justice, Feldman says, "Well, of course, the *Roberson* Court said it was applying an old rule, and we can always say that. But remember, we also can always say we are applying a new rule. We are, after all, postmodern."[14] Viewed this way, the habeas/retroactivity discussion conducted by the Rehnquist Court looks like an instrumental use of doctrine to reach a pre-given result, rather than a careful and impartial analysis. Rules of language create space for a range of meanings, and the Court utilized that space to forge its desired result. That result came with concrete, life-or-death results for habeas petitioners during the Court's tenure.

Other Early Rehnquist Court Habeas Rulings

Coleman v. Thompson (1991)[15] narrowed the precedent of a Warren Court decision, *Fay v. Noia*, that was discussed in chapter 5. In *Coleman*, the Supreme Court refused to review a federal question decided by a state court because there was an "independent state ground" for the ruling. Here, the states' rights and government power preferences of Rehnquist's jurisprudence converged. Rehnquist did not write the opinion, but he joined it.

Keeney v. Tamayo-Reyes (1992)[16] also revisited a Warren Court ruling. This time, the issue was what standard must be met in order to receive an evidentiary hearing in a habeas proceeding. The petitioner claimed that he did not understand the explanation of "manslaughter" that was given before he entered his guilty plea because he did not speak English. The Court denied petitioner an evidentiary hearing, finding that this error, which resulted from defense counsel's negligence, was not sufficiently significant to entitle him to a hearing.

Brecht v. Abramson (1993)[17] raised the question of defining "harmless error" in a murder trial. The Supreme Court ruled that less certainty was required on collateral review (i.e., in habeas cases) than on direct appeal when the state sought to show that a trial error was harmless. This rule made it easier to defeat habeas claims because an error could be deemed harmless without proving it to be so beyond a reasonable doubt.

Actual Innocence as Grounds for Habeas Relief: Herrera v. Collins *(1993)*

A habeas case decided in 1993 raised concerns for civil liberties advocates because it seemed to suggest that the Rehnquist Court found it acceptable for states to execute prisoners who might be innocent.[18] *Herrera v. Collins* was guaranteed to generate controversy from the start, as it arose out of the murder of two police officers in Texas. The first officer, Rucker, was found dead outside of his patrol car, and the second (Carrisalez) was shot after he pulled over a motorist for speeding. Defendant Herrera was convicted of the murder of Carrisalez and then pleaded guilty to the murder of Rucker. He was sentenced to death.

After he had exhausted his appeals and with his execution date approaching, Herrera filed a federal petition for habeas corpus. In support of his petition, he submitted several affidavits from individuals claiming that Herrera's late brother had committed the murders, and that the brother had confessed to both killings as well. Thus, Herrera argued, execution of an innocent person would violate the Eighth and Fourteenth Amendments. The district court agreed to grant an evidentiary hearing, but the Court of Appeals for the Fifth Circuit overturned that ruling. The Supreme Court sided with the Fifth Circuit, and the state proceeded with the execution. Herrera went to the death chamber proclaiming his innocence to the end.

In his majority opinion, Justice Rehnquist emphasized that habeas corpus may be used to challenge a conviction only when there is an underlying constitutional violation. Simply asserting one's innocence is not enough to obtain habeas relief. In support of this statement of law, the opinion cites a Warren Court habeas case, *Townsend v. Sain*. There, the Court said:

> Where newly discovered evidence is alleged in a habeas application, evidence which could not reasonably have been presented to the state trier of facts, the federal court must grant an evidentiary hearing. Of course, such evidence must bear upon the constitutionality of the applicant's detention; the existence merely of newly discovered evidence relevant to the guilt of a state prisoner is not a ground for relief on federal habeas corpus.[19]

This citation to a Warren Court opinion was strategic, for it suggested that even the pro-defendant Warren Court would not go so far as to embrace Herrera's position. But the statement was only dictum (i.e., a statement extraneous to the court's ruling and unnecessary to the decision) in a case where the Court actually *did* order an evidentiary hearing. Also, Herrera *was* in fact making a constitutional argument. He contended that the execution of an innocent person violated both the Eighth Amendment's prohibition on cruel and unusual punishment and the Fourteenth Amendment's Due Process Clause.

The majority in *Herrera* was confronting a difficult problem in criminal jurisprudence: How can a court be sure that the person facing punishment is not innocent? No one wants to say that it is acceptable to punish an innocent person, of course, and so courts deflect the question of innocence by focusing on other things: on the "full and fair trial below," or on the burden-shifting that occurs after conviction. Rehnquist acknowledges that innocence matters in the process when he says that courts do not turn a "blind eye"[20] toward innocence, and he "assume[s] for the sake of argument" that "a truly persuasive demonstration of 'actual innocence' made after trial would render the execution of a defendant unconstitutional."[21] Rehnquist does not specify what standard such a "truly persuasive demonstration" would have to meet, but he says in a conclusory way that Herrera failed to meet it.

The *Herrera* decision also makes petitioner's constitutional claim dependent on whether or not there are state law avenues to relief available. Executive clemency is such an avenue, the majority says. The governor could pardon Herrera or grant him clemency, and that possibility is enough to amount to an alternative state law procedure that obviates the need for the Supreme Court to act. Of course, clemency is always theoretically available, but it varies from state to state, and it is a discretionary (and political) decision rather than an adjudicated one. Put another way, clemency amounts to the relinquishment by the executive of a right it would otherwise have to detain a person. It is unappealable and final. Counting clemency as a legal alternative to habeas relief for the innocent is inaccurate, if not disingenuous.

In denying Herrera a hearing, Rehnquist leans heavily on the law enforcement interest in the finality of criminal judgments. He says that "in any system of criminal justice, 'innocence' or 'guilt' must be determined in some sort of a judicial proceeding."[22] He is arguing here for the finality of convictions. But one can easily turn that argument around and say that innocence can *only* be established in a judicial proceeding. In other words, a hearing is required in order for a petitioner to demonstrate innocence and gain release from state custody. So by choosing to emphasize the judicial determination of guilt, the majority de-emphasizes the importance of a judicial ruling on evidence of actual innocence that would have been made in a habeas proceeding.

Justice Blackmun filed an angry dissent in *Herrera*. Unlike the majority, he would find a constitutional basis, in both the Eighth and the Fourteenth Amendment, for the prohibition on executing an innocent person. Because the case law defines cruel and unusual punishment in terms of "evolving standards of decency," Blackmun applies that standard, and he finds the execution of an innocent person to be "at odds with any standard of decency that I can imagine."[23] In addition to that Eighth Amendment right, he finds a Fourteenth Amendment violation in the execution of an innocent person. It would violate substantive due process because executing an innocent person "shocks the conscience." Blackmun compares the case to *Rochin v. California* (1952), in which the police pumped a suspect's stomach to obtain evidence of drug possession. There, the Court found the police conduct shocking to the conscience and therefore violative of substantive due process. The police conduct in *Rochin* was, the Court said, "too close to the rack and the screw."[24]

Blackmun also faults the majority for failing to state what the threshold for an actual innocence claim would be. As noted earlier, the majority opinion suggests that a "truly persuasive showing" of innocence might raise a constitutional issue, but it provides no standard for making such a showing. Thus, the statement is of no use to a petitioner seeking to establish actual innocence. Blackmun cites a well-known article by Judge Friendly to suggest that concern with innocence is a key element of habeas corpus jurisprudence. Although Friendly was arguing for limitation of postconviction review, he thought that actual innocence claims were the most compelling variety.[25] Thus, Blackmun suggested, innocence claims should receive the closest scrutiny rather than the most perfunctory. Blackmun also derides the majority's reliance on executive clemency as a legal remedy. In the end, he states his problem with the majority opinion in emphatic terms. "The execution of a person who can show that he is innocent," he says, "comes perilously close to simple murder."[26]

Herrera was divisive and controversial because it spoke directly to the core concern of the criminal justice system: separating the guilty from the innocent. The majority cited the need to bring criminal proceedings to a close and to cut off challenges at some point in the process. They assured the public that they did not doubt petitioner's guilt. However, by denying him the opportunity to present evidence of his innocence at a hearing, they left open the possibility that he could demonstrate his innocence to the satisfaction of the trial judge (who had ordered such a hearing but was reversed on appeal). Of course, it is important to remember that Herrera was not seeking immediate release but an evidentiary hearing in which he could *prove* that he was entitled to release. It was quite possible that the district judge would have adjudged the evidence insufficient to establish innocence. We will never know, of course. The problem of certainty in criminal punishment will always be with us, but the majority in *Herrera* drew the line terminating judicial review of criminal cases too far from certainty, leaving a haunting question about whether an innocent person was executed—and making it more likely that such outcomes would occur in the future. Herrera's story raises the core concern that prompted the drafting of the Magna Carta's Article 39 in the first place: that a prisoner receive the protection of the "law of the land" before being deprived of life or liberty. But the Court found a way to interpret the law of the land/due process that barred the prisoner from showing his innocence.

New Legislative Restrictions on Habeas Corpus: The AEDPA

The AEDPA was passed in 1996, a year after the bombing of the Oklahoma City federal building that killed 168 people, including 19 children.[27] The act was designed, as its name suggests, to combat terrorism and to facilitate punishment for those convicted of violent crimes. A major objective of the law was to curtail federal habeas corpus rights. One way that the AEDPA did this was by codifying the rule against new rules first stated in *Teague v. Lane*, discussed earlier. The AEDPA also placed limits on successive habeas petitions and precluded Supreme Court review of certain habeas petitions denied below.[28] It created an evidentiary presumption in favor of government that could only be rebutted by clear and convincing evidence.

The AEDPA resulted most directly from the horrific attack in Oklahoma City. The loss of life, the scale of destruction, and the defiance shown by the principal defendant, Timothy McVeigh, all contributed to the sense of public outrage that followed in the wake of the April 1995 bombing. In fact, some provisions of the AEDPA refer directly to the use of explosives as part of a terrorist act. Congress began work on what would ultimately become the AEDPA immediately after the attack.

Despite this relationship between the Oklahoma City bombing and the new law, it is striking to note how much of the Rehnquist Court's habeas jurisprudence was fixed in positive (statutory) law by the AEDPA. When Congress decided to respond to the tragedy with new legislation, a blueprint for restricting habeas corpus was ready at hand. Thus, the relationship between Congress and the Court was not a back-and-forth, dialogical one (as, for instance, we see in the post-9/11 detainee cases discussed in chapter 7) but a statutory reinforcement of doctrinal positions already laid out by the Court. This convergence of national mood and the Court's ideological inclination was greatly intensified by the terrorist act in Oklahoma City, which produced a demand for urgent action. Ironically, perhaps, the habeas corpus provisions of the AEDPA did not relate to the bombing; they were a part of the legislation that advanced other law enforcement interests. As Anthony Gregory has noted, the AEDPA vastly expands federal power in some ways (e.g., immigration enforcement) while facilitating *state* power in others (e.g., finality of state court judgments).[29]

Innocence Claims Post-Rehnquist: District Attorney's Office v. Osborne *(2009)*

William Rehnquist died in 2005, and John Roberts succeeded him as chief justice. The question whether proof of actual innocence entitles a postconviction prisoner to a habeas hearing continues to arise in the present era of sophisticated DNA testing. In recent years, a number of prisoners have been freed after DNA testing proved with certainty or near certainty that they were innocent. The Innocence Project developed due in large part to the new capabilities of DNA testing technology to conclusively resolve factual questions involving physical evidence, and many other organizations throughout the country today pursue a similar mission.[30] But this focus on DNA testing has raised a range of questions for policy makers and judges. Some of these questions have to do with the finality of state court judgments—a concern that weighs heavily in the estimation of pro–law enforcement commentators and officials. They suggest that if access to habeas, or the notion of due process, were to be broadened, every convicted prisoner would prolong their challenges to their convictions, depriving the state and its citizens of a final result in the prosecution process and requiring vast and unnecessary expenditures of state resources. Thus, it is best, according to this view, to leave the regulation of prisoners' requests for DNA testing in the hands of state legislatures, which are best equipped to balance cost, public safety, and prisoners' rights. Positive law made by the legislatures, rather than adjudication of rights claims by the courts, would be the preferable means of fashioning standards to regulate the growing number and variety of DNA-related arguments in the criminal justice process.

The DNA testing debate raises the innocence issue once again, and at its core the recent dispute proceeds from the same tension observable in the earlier habeas cases decided by the Rehnquist Court: concern about executing (or imprisoning) the innocent versus the need for finality in criminal prosecutions. In 2009, the Supreme Court ruled on an Alaska case where the petitioner had been convicted at trial and had exhausted his direct appeals but later sought to obtain DNA testing to prove his factual innocence. This was not actually a habeas case: petitioner (Osborne) was requesting DNA material that was in state custody as trial evidence. Once he obtained test results, he would then have presumably made a habeas petition based on the fact that the state was holding him in custody when he was in fact innocent of any crime. The state denied his request for the DNA sample, and he commenced a Section 1983 action,[31] claiming that the state had violated his due process rights by denying his request for the DNA. The 1983 action was intended to demonstrate innocence upon which a subsequent habeas petition would then be predicated. The U.S. District Court ruled in Osborne's favor, and the Ninth Circuit affirmed that ruling. However, the Supreme Court reversed the lower court and found in favor of the state. The majority ruled that there was no due process violation in the state's refusal to allow Osborne to access the DNA trial evidence. In their view, the dispute posed a choice between recognition of a new, broad due process right in the postconviction setting and deference to state legislatures to set workable limits to DNA testing postconviction. They chose the latter option, declining to take up the due process question and essentially conceptualizing the dispute as a political question.

Justice Stevens dissented. He had two problems with the majority opinion. He argued, first, that Osborne had a due process right arising out of the state-created postconviction procedures. The state had not properly followed its own procedures, so that Osborne was deprived of procedural due process at the postconviction review stage. Second, this was also a clear-cut instance where a *substantive* liberty interest was present but not recognized. With regard to the substantive due process claim, Stevens cited the long lineage of due process–related liberty: "The liberty protected by the Due Process Clause is not a creation of the Bill of Rights. Indeed, our Nation has long recognized that the liberty safeguarded by the Constitution has far deeper roots. See Declaration of Independence ¶2 (holding it self-evident that 'all men are . . . endowed by their Creator with certain unalienable Rights,' among which are 'Life, Liberty, and the pursuit of Happiness.')."[32]

Stevens also tied his due process argument to the *Hamdi* case, which had been decided five years earlier: "The 'most elemental' of the liberties protected by the Due Process Clause is 'the interest in being free from physical detention by one's own government.' *Hamdi v. Rumsfeld*, 542 U. S. 507, 529 (2004) (plurality opinion)."[33] The petitioner needed access to the DNA in order to show that it did not come from him. This, to Stevens, was a quintessential assertion of a liberty interest because the evidence sought was instrumental to gaining freedom from confinement. Though *Osborne* was not a habeas case, the core concern and result were the same: the petitioner sought a chance to prove his innocence postconviction, and he was denied that opportunity. The gravamen of *Herrera v. Collins*—that proof of innocence alone does not entitle a petitioner to postconviction relief—applied with equal force sixteen years later, indicating that the effects of the Rehnquist Court's constriction of habeas corpus were felt even after the Rehnquist era had passed.

Conclusion

Steven Smith sums up the impact of the Rehnquist Court on the law of habeas corpus by comparing it to the Warren Court's orientation:

> [The Warren Court's] broad, remedial vision of habeas corpus survived the Burger years, if not unscathed, at least intact. The Rehnquist Court, however, buried it in a single case, *Teague v. Lane*. There, the Court held that habeas corpus should be available only to deter egregious misconduct by state courts, a far narrower role than remedying constitutional errors. Henceforth, habeas corpus would only be used to enforce "old" law, barring claims seeking "new law" in habeas cases except in truly extraordinary circumstances.[34]

And yet when he asks, rhetorically, who "won" the battle between the Warren Court and the Rehnquist Court for establishing a legacy in criminal procedure, Smith answers his own question by saying that both did. Warren won because "criminal procedure remains thoroughly constitutionalized, with rules of federal constitutional law covering virtually every aspect of the criminal justice system."[35] But Rehnquist also won:

> Disfavored Warren Court doctrines were altered through case-by-case adjudication so that they no longer threatened

> what Rehnquist and his "law and order" colleagues regarded as "legitimate law enforcement." The results have been dramatic: much evidence that the Warren Court would have suppressed under *Miranda* or *Mapp* now comes into evidence again, and habeas petitions that might have been successful even a generation ago are now doomed to failure. Thanks to the Rehnquist Court, in short, things are again rosy for law enforcement.[36]

This judgment does not mean, of course, that every Supreme Court decision rendered between 1986 and 2005 was antidefendant or restrictive of habeas corpus. After all, each justice had his or her individual views on legal questions, and the chief did not command a majority for each and every ruling. This is always the case with any incarnation of the Supreme Court one chooses to examine, throughout the Court's history. It is possible, however, to speak of the general orientation of the Rehnquist Court, just as it was possible to do with the Taney Court, the Warren Court, and others. The habeas decisions discussed here constitute one significant part of Rehnquist's legacy, and they were solidified by the passage of the AEDPA, which codified some of the case law immediately preceding it. And the fact that Rehnquist and like-minded fellow justices were willing to take on Warren precedents to criticize or even reject them lends greater historical significance to the Court's two decades of criminal procedure rulings. The Court revisited *Fay v. Noia* and charted a different course for separating out state law issues on federal habeas. In his article on habeas corpus, Judge Friendly argued that the *Fay* Court actually misread English history and overstated the force of habeas as well as the English courts' willingness to use it. No matter who is right on the history here, it remains true that habeas took on new doctrinal developments in the United States. In writing the opinion in *Fay v. Noia*, Justice Brennan claimed an essential meaning for habeas corpus arising out of English legal history. According to that conception, habeas was a fundamental and crucial restraint on the government's power to detain. There were key historical differences between early modern England and the United States. For one, the configuration of power among Crown, people, and Parliament was particular to England, and at times habeas figured in the power struggles between the two political branches. Gregory shows that the passage of the Habeas Corpus Act of 1679 was motivated in part by concerns about the practice of hauling one's political enemies into court, and that Parliament suspended the writ during the Glorious Revolution.[37] The United States, too, had its particularities that inflected habeas development. The use of habeas by both sides in the struggle over slavery showed both the importance of habeas corpus as a means to asserting liberty and the limits of the writ in times of deep political conflict, as Gregory also notes.[38]

The Rehnquist Court restricted the availability of habeas corpus by limiting the claims that could be made, compressing the time frames for making them, requiring deference to the states on evidentiary questions, and privileging finality over individual rights. Congress helped this effort by codifying those changes in the AEDPA. It is no coincidence that executions continued at a brisk rate during this period, and prison populations swelled.

The story does not end here, of course. Habeas corpus—a central legacy of the Magna Carta—figured prominently in the struggle over detainee policy post-9/11. The executive sought, with Congress's eventual help, to place its "war on terror" detainees beyond the reach of the courts, and the Court turned to habeas corpus to rebuff that effort. Habeas review became less meaningful for detainees once the Supreme Court backed away from involvement in the development of habeas case law post-2008, but the resuscitation of the writ was nonetheless important in the course of case law development. That is one of the themes to be taken up in the following chapter on common law constitutionalism in the war on terror.

7

The War on Terror

Magna Carta decreed that no man would be imprisoned contrary to the law of the land.

Justice Anthony Kennedy in *Boumediene v. Bush* (2008)

The Constitution would not require the government to provide further process to such a U.S. citizen before using lethal force.

Department of Justice white paper explaining legal authority for drone strikes

The years following the 9/11 attacks saw U.S. policy makers questioning fundamental assumptions about the limits of state power and the treatment of individuals. Commentators forthrightly advocated torture and justified it in consequentialist terms. American intelligence personnel used coercive interrogation against terrorist suspects and sent other suspects overseas for interrogation by governments that practiced torture. The United States captured and imprisoned suspected enemy combatants, often with very little supporting evidence, and held them for long periods. Lethal targeted strikes were carried out against specific terrorist leaders, including a U.S. citizen. These government actions showed that the United States saw the post-9/11 world as fundamentally different, requiring new responses to global terrorism as well as a rethinking of previously honored prohibitions on government conduct.

Yet even in this new context, the Supreme Court continued to invoke the Magna Carta tradition of restraint on executive power, just as it had done at the other critical junctures examined in this book. As it engaged in dialogue with the political branches between 2004 and 2008, the Court referenced the Magna Carta explicitly as a still-relevant source of authority limiting the executive's ability to detain. In two cases that will be discussed in this chapter, *Rasul v. Bush* and *Boumediene v. Bush*, the majority opinion relied specifically and directly on the Magna Carta to support its pro–individual rights holding. These references show the continuing relevance of the Magna Carta in U.S. law, but they also demonstrate the vitality of common law constitutionalism. The Suspension Clause of the U.S. Constitution references habeas corpus, and the *Rasul* and *Boumediene* rulings link habeas corpus to the "law of the land" provision of the Magna Carta's Article 39. The Court draws here on the historical and traditional significance of that older provision in the struggle against government power, making a link between constitutional text and the traditions lying behind it.

Reviewing the record of post-9/11 court decisions, including those rendered by the Supreme Court, it is clear that the judiciary has frequently been deferential to claims of executive authority. It would be inaccurate to say that the courts have unswervingly stood up against the executive's efforts to curtail individual liberties by detention, blocking access to the courts, or targeted killing. Nonetheless, the rulings that *have* rebuffed such attempts remain important, and they have resulted in part from a willingness to look at constitutional text in a way that incorporates traditions of individual rights protection. It is not inconsistent to claim, on the one hand, that the courts have not always been willing to check executive power in the war on terror, and, on the other hand, that they have at times issued important rulings that *do* provide such a check. The decisional record indicates evidence of both.

In this chapter, I will explore the role of the Magna Carta in legal disputes arising post-9/11. These disputes fall broadly into three categories: (1) questions of access to the federal courts, (2) questions concerning interrogation standards, and (3) procedures due to be followed prior to using lethal force against an individual. All three categories relate to the Magna Carta: the first by reference to habeas corpus, and the second and third by virtue of due process (law of the land).

Procedural Obstacles to Challenging Detention: Blocking Access to the Federal Courts

Immediately following the attacks of 9/11, the U.S. government began capturing and detaining people it suspected of having ties to al-Qaeda. The government then faced the problem of what to do with these prisoners. Where would they be held, and for how long? What procedures applied to their processing and treatment? There is a long-standing distinction between detaining people for committing crimes and capturing prisoners on the battlefield. The former group fall within the control of civil authorities administering the criminal justice system. The latter group have traditionally been considered prisoners of war, who remain under the control of military authorities. A criminal defendant's procedural rights are enumerated in the Bill of Rights, and they include the right to a speedy trial, a jury of one's peers, legal representation, and cross-examination of adverse witnesses. Additionally, a defendant can appeal after conviction up through the state or federal system and ultimately can ask the U.S. Supreme Court to review the case. And habeas corpus is also available. Habeas corpus, as we have seen, is the ancient writ that allows a government prisoner to petition for release from illegal confinement. Habeas relief can be sought at any time during a defendant's incarceration—even after all other appeals have been exhausted. Habeas is not an "appeal," strictly speaking, but a challenge to the government's legal authority to hold a prisoner. Thus, it focuses on the legality of detention rather than the conduct of trial. It can also be used to seek release from confinement when no charges have been brought.

Prisoners of war face a different set of procedures. They fall under military jurisdiction, and therefore their treatment is governed by the Uniform Code of Military Justice (UCMJ).[1] The UCMJ sets forth requirements for various proceedings related to military operations, including courts-martial used to try military offenses. The requirements of the UCMJ differ from those of civilian criminal courts. The UCMJ also incorporates the provisions of the Geneva Conventions related to prisoner treatment. When the Bush administration categorized its detainees at Guantanamo and elsewhere as "unlawful enemy combatants," it was seeking to avoid the application of the UCMJ and the Geneva Conventions to those captives. The detainees were held for long periods of time (years, in many cases) but never charged with an offense. In November 2001, President Bush had issued a military order declaring that suspected terrorists who were non–U.S. citizens would not have access to civilian courts to challenge their detention. They would be tried by special military commissions operating under rules set by the administration. In practice, though, some of the detainees would not be charged at all, and so their detention was open-ended.

The Supreme Court ruled four times on detainee treatment between 2004 and 2008, and these rulings show a back-and-forth struggle between the Court on one side and the executive and legislative branches on the other. After each ruling, the Bush administration sought to circumvent the decision by procedural change. First, *Hamdi v. Rumsfeld* (2004) presented the question whether the administration could detain a U.S. citizen terror suspect without criminal charges as part of the war on terror. The Court found this detention lawful because it fell within the authority granted by Congress in September 2001, when it passed the Authorization for Use of Military Force (AUMF). The Court deemed the AUMF sufficient to empower the executive to detain prisoners without charges as part of the war effort. However, the Court also said that "the state of war is not a blank check for the executive."[2] It required that the government provide procedural protections to the detainees, including some type of fact-finding hearing prior to classifying a detainee as an enemy combatant. Thus, the *Hamdi* decision conceptualized due process in a flexible, open way: it varied according to context and could be adapted as new situations (such as the war on terror) arose. But while such flexibility had been a part of common law constitutionalism in the past, it turned out not to be a liberty-enhancing development in the detainees' rights context because it allowed the executive to devise and implement one-sided and self-serving hearing procedures.

In response to the *Hamdi* decision, the administration began using Combatant Status Review Tribunals (CSRTs) as the sole forum for challenging one's classification as an enemy combatant. The CSRT was an internal military proceeding meant to substitute for a court hearing, although the proceedings were nowhere near what would have been available to an ordinary criminal defendant in civilian court and in fact were virtually impossible to win. Mark Denbeaux and Joshua Denbeaux studied the records of CSRT proceedings. Information they obtained from the Defense Department through Freedom of Information Act (FOIA) requests and in the course of habeas proceedings depicts a hearing process that falls far short of fundamental procedural fairness. In a report entitled *No-Hearing Hearings*, Denbeaux and Denbeaux present data on 558 CSRT hearings.[3] Among many striking statistics, the authors report that in 96 percent of the cases for which information was available, "the

Government did not produce any witnesses in any hearing and did not present any documentary evidence to the detainee prior to the hearing."[4] Moreover, all defense requests to call witnesses from outside Guantanamo were denied, and 74 percent of defense requests to call witnesses who were *inside* Guantanamo were also denied. Although a personal representative (instead of a lawyer) was assigned to each detainee at the hearing, those individuals frequently failed to participate, and they sometimes advocated for the government.[5]

Despite the difficulties facing the detainee at a CSRT hearing, three of the cases that Denbeaux and Denbeaux surveyed did, in fact, result in a finding that the detainee was not, or was no longer, an enemy combatant.[6] Thus, three detainees were able to surmount the difficult procedural obstacles and establish that their detention was improper, even by the government's own standard. However, two of the three victorious individuals were reexamined at a second CSRT and found to be enemy combatants. The third victorious individual actually won a *second* hearing as well—at which point he was ordered adjudicated a third time. The third time, he lost and was declared an enemy combatant.

Clearly, the CSRT hearings did not represent the meaningful opportunity to contest one's classification as an enemy combatant that the Supreme Court had required in its *Hamdi* ruling. Meanwhile, the Supreme Court ruled on a related issue in *Rasul v. Bush* (2004). There, the Court decided that procedural protections specified by the federal habeas corpus statute were available to Guantanamo detainees, including noncitizens.[7] This ruling was an important precursor to the *Boumediene* decision four years later. In *Rasul*, Justice Stevens cited the Magna Carta by quoting an earlier opinion by Justice Jackson at length:

> "Executive imprisonment has been considered oppressive and lawless since John, at Runnymede, pledged that no free man should be imprisoned, dispossessed, outlawed, or

> exiled save by the judgment of his peers or by the law of the land. The judges of England developed the writ of habeas corpus largely to preserve these immunities from executive restraint." *Shaughnessy v. United States ex rel. Mezei*, 345 U.S. 206, 218–219 (1953) (dissenting opinion).[8]

Determined to keep the detainees from reaching the federal courts, the Bush administration successfully lobbied Congress to pass the Detainee Treatment Act (DTA) of 2005.[9] That law stripped the federal courts of jurisdiction over the detainees' legal claims and, in particular, prevented the detainees from seeking habeas relief there. The law was challenged by another detainee, Salim Hamdan, who faced a military commission trial on conspiracy charges. In *Hamdan v. Rumsfeld*, the Supreme Court dealt another rebuke to the Bush administration by ruling that the military commission seeking to try Hamdan was not properly constituted when judged by the UCMJ as it then existed.[10] The Court also ruled that Hamdan's case in the federal courts was not foreclosed by the jurisdiction-stripping language of the DTA. In response to this decision, the administration went back to Congress once again and obtained passage of the Military Commissions Act (MCA) of 2006.[11] The MCA authorized military commissions of the sort that the administration wanted to use, and it was free once again, it seemed, to do so.

The Boumediene *Ruling and Its Aftermath*

Finally, in *Boumediene v. Bush* (2008), the Court squarely faced the constitutional question of the availability of habeas relief for detainees. The administration had tried to foreclose that option, first by military order and then by urging legislative action. Now, the Court had to decide whether these attempts to block access to the courts violated the Constitution. Article I, Section

9, Clause 2 states, "The privilege of the Writ of Habeas Corpus shall not be suspended, unless when in the Cases of Rebellion or Invasion the public Safety shall require it." From this language, which appears in Article I's grant of power to Congress, it is clear that only Congress may suspend the writ of habeas corpus. Did the MCA's jurisdiction-stripping provision amount to a suspension? The Court ruled that it did not. Unless Congress specifically intended to suspend the writ, rather than simply foreclosing its availability to a particular group of potential habeas petitioners, suspension had not been accomplished by the MCA, and the writ remained operative. And CSRT hearings were not an adequate substitute for habeas corpus proceedings. The Court found, further, that the reach of habeas corpus extended to the U.S. base at Guantanamo Bay, even though that base was located outside the United States, on the territory of the sovereign nation of Cuba. The end result of this decision was to require the federal courts to hear and decide habeas corpus petitions filed by the detainees remaining at Guantanamo. The doors of the federal courts were now open to them, and they could seek the ultimate remedy habeas provided: release from state custody. And in making this important ruling, the Court made reference once again to the Magna Carta. Habeas corpus, Justice Kennedy said, "became the means by which the promise of Magna Carta was fulfilled."[12] This linkage allowed the Court to justify its requirement that habeas corpus remain available to Guantanamo detainees. The right of habeas corpus for prisoners in other locations, such as Afghanistan, has not been recognized by the courts.

Baher Azmy has shown that the *Boumediene* decision generated a "new common law of habeas."[13] Once the Supreme Court found in *Boumediene* that Guantanamo detainees were entitled to petition for habeas corpus, the number of those petitions lodged with the federal courts multiplied, and the courts needed to develop procedural and substantive decisional rules they could apply consistently as litigants presented habeas petitions for review. This was common law in the sense of judge-made law, and federal judges were making it upon a new legal landscape. How should "enemy combatant" be defined? What should the standard of proof be? Did the burden shift at some point to require the detainee to rebut the government's allegations? Should hearsay be allowed? Did evidence of torture disqualify confession?

Benjamin Wittes, Robert Chesney, and Larkin Reynolds have compiled a comprehensive report on post-*Boumediene* case law and have updated it periodically. The report addresses the questions raised here, and it indicates frequent divergence among the approaches of district court judges, as well as correction of district court rulings, in some instances, by the D.C. Circuit. Close reading of the decisions does show some broad agreement on rules, though, particularly after the D.C. Circuit handed down instructions. One example involves conditional probability analysis, also called "mosaic theory."[14] The district court judges were initially skeptical of the government's use of mosaic theory to support detention, but the D.C. Circuit issued instructions on appeal directing the lower court to accept that theory. Originally a concept used in intelligence analysis, mosaic theory suggests that bits of evidence (or "tiles" in a mosaic) that seem insignificant standing alone can gain greater explanatory force when viewed as part of a larger pattern, or mosaic. The usefulness of this theory in intelligence analysis seems intuitively plausible, but when transposed to the evidentiary context, mosaic theory can be problematic. As District Judge Kessler put it, "The kind and amount of evidence which satisfies the intelligence community in reaching final conclusions about the value of information it obtains may be very different, and certainly cannot govern the Court's ruling."[15] Kessler and other district court judges were concerned about the *quality* of evidence constituting the mosaic. She went on to explain:

> Even using the Government's theoretical model of a mosaic, it must be acknowledged that the mosaic theory is only as persuasive as the tiles which compose it and the glue which binds them together—just as a brick wall is only as strong as the individual bricks which support it and the cement that keeps the bricks in place. Therefore, if the individual pieces of a mosaic are inherently flawed or do not fit together, then the mosaic will split apart, just as the brick wall will collapse.[16]

The individual pieces of evidence in that case were "inherently flawed" in the court's view; their probity was in question. As a result, the court rejected the government's mosaic (by which it sought to justify detention of the habeas petitioner) and granted the habeas petition.

On appeal, the D.C. Circuit took a very different view, rebuking the district court for misunderstanding probability analysis and directing it to analyze the evidence in habeas cases using the mosaic theory offered by the government. The "mistake" committed by the lower court—and repeated by other district judges—was to apply evidentiary standards to each piece of evidence, such that each one had to be competent, relevant, and material.[17] The appellate judges on the D.C. Circuit instructed the lower court to view the evidentiary picture as a mosaic rather than as discrete pieces of evidence—which is to say, more like an intelligence analyst than a judicial tribunal. But this directive shortchanged the historical function of habeas courts. Throughout the history of the writ, the courts' ideal role has been to check executive power, not to facilitate it. The post-*Boumediene* habeas proceedings are not the first time, of course, that courts hearing habeas petitions have fallen short of their ideal functioning and failed to stand up against executive detention. Nonetheless, it is easy to see how the D.C. Circuit's midcourse correction on evidentiary review represents a step backward in the development of the "new common law of habeas." On appeal, the court is more concerned about protecting the government's interest and vindicating its intelligence judgment than ensuring procedural accuracy and fairness. The government's interest here is weighty: no one would dispute that. Yet the court's institutional role is different from the executive's. To blur these institutional lines is to deviate from the tradition cited by the Supreme Court in *Rasul* and *Boumediene* in which the courts provide relief from unlawful executive detention.

In his *Al-Adahi* opinion reinstating the mosaic theory, Judge Randolph spoke at length about the difference between independent versus related probabilities, accusing the lower court of misunderstanding that difference. Independent events (e.g., individual coin flips) can be considered in isolation, when one is estimating probability, because one such event does not make another one more likely. Related events, by contrast, do affect each other in probability terms: a person who is very tall is also more likely to be above average in weight. Thus, Judge Randolph suggests, the lower court erred by looking at each piece of evidence in isolation rather than as a composite.[18] This was a sort of "mosaic theory writ large," in the sense that it was not only about what the evidence in this case meant but also about the proper way to review evidence in general. Associated events raise probabilities, the court seemed to say: if X and Y are common characteristics of terrorists, then a suspect who exemplifies both X *and* Y is more likely to be a terrorist than one who simply exhibits X *but not* Y. Once again, though, the concern is that the individual pieces of evidence are not competent: they resulted from torture or were compound hearsay. The question of whether they should be evidence at all arises prior to the question of how they should be analyzed. But once the D.C. Circuit ruled on the mosaic theory, it sent a clear message to the court below. And, as Wittes et al. put it, "The district-court judges are now very cognizant of the new instructions from the D.C. Circuit."[19]

In other respects, too, the "emerging law of detention" fashioned by the federal courts hearing habeas petitions has become less favorable to habeas petitioners. The standard of proof in detainee habeas cases generally is "preponderance of the evidence," so that the government has merely to show that the petitioners' membership in a terrorist group is more likely than not. Although some petitioners argued for a higher standard of proof, they were unsuccessful. In fact, the court has said that not even a preponderance standard is required by the Supreme Court's *Boumediene* decision, so that even that standard might conceivably be lowered.[20] Similarly, the question of what effect coercion has on evidentiary value is unsettled. Although the D.C. Circuit has not yet ruled on the level or type of coercion that would render a confession or other statement inadmissible, the court has said that violation of the Geneva Conventions would not, by itself, make such evidence excludable.[21] These judge-made limitations on detainee habeas relief have made the *Boumediene* victory an empty one for many petitioners. Wittes et al. have calculated that thirty-eight petitioners had been granted relief as of the spring of 2012. Of those, seventeen related to a specific ethnic group (Chinese Uighurs) who were distinguishable from other cases because they were not actually habeas cases.[22] Thus, only twenty-one petitions were actually granted, and fourteen of those were not appealed by the government. Of the remaining seven that the government did appeal, all were overturned (the government prevailed on appeal) or remanded after appeal. Perhaps most strikingly, the D.C. Circuit (the federal appellate court) had not ruled even once in favor of a detainee on the merits of a case.[23]

In June 2012, the Supreme Court declined to review the D.C. Circuit's denial of habeas relief to seven Guantanamo detainees.[24] These were petitioners who had challenged their detention via a petition for habeas corpus but lost. They had taken advantage of the *Boumediene* ruling by filing habeas petitions, but habeas relief was denied. Because the Supreme Court did not review their habeas denials, the petitioners were left without further avenues to seek relief, and the adverse rulings became final. The Court seemed to be signaling that it would take a "hands-off" approach to the habeas proceedings in the lower federal courts, leading commentators to speculate that the Court would weaken the effect of the *Boumediene* ruling by leaving the lower courts to formulate their own, restrictive standards for habeas cases.[25]

In the end, then, the procedural devices employed by the Bush and Obama administrations were effective in preventing challenges to detention policy in the war on terror. Initially, petitioners were unable to access the courts—their only available forum was the CSRT hearing. These proceedings were structured and operated to create maximum disadvantage for the detainees. Congressional action kept the detainees from getting into court until the 2008 *Boumediene* ruling declaring them eligible to petition for habeas corpus relief. Even then, the lower courts' rulings were deferential to the military authorities who classified detainees as enemy combatants in the first place. When the Supreme Court let those rulings stand, habeas corpus became in those cases a right without a remedy.

In the fall of 2013, as the War in Afghanistan reached an end, new questions arose regarding the status of the remaining Guantanamo detainees. No new prisoners had arrived in five years, and the ones still detained had been there as long as twelve years.[26] With the war ending, the 2001 Authorization for Use of Military Force, which provided the legal basis for the war on terror, might be revoked. Without the AUMF, the executive's legal authority to hold detainees is questionable. This eventuality could give rise to new habeas challenges in the future. At present, though, it is clear that the law of procedure has been successfully managed by the political branches to prevent the detainees from successfully challenging their confinement. And the concern raised by the Supreme Court—that the Magna Carta's "law of the land" provision was not being honored—remains a very real one.

Interrogation Methods and the Torture Prohibition

The 9/11 attacks brought "torture" into everyday discourse. As the ultimate illiberal state action, torture is generally anathema to those who believe in the importance of civil liberties and the rule of law. Nonetheless, the fear and anger produced by the attacks led some people to rethink the torture prohibition. If it yielded a greater good, such as averting another mass attack, might torture be defensible on consequentialist grounds? The circumstances of the post-9/11 world generated questions of substantive law concerning how terror suspects should be treated. The Bush administration took a number of legal and rhetorical steps to give itself flexibility in using torture methods against terror suspects. Of course, the use of torture would be denounced officially, while interrogation methods actually in use were defined as not-torture. Also, individuals could be "rendered" to overseas locations where foreign governments used any interrogation method they chose and then provided the fruits of that interrogation to the United States. Vice President Cheney called this the "dark side"—which, incidentally, also became the title of an excellent book on the rendition program.[27]

The United States acknowledged using coercive interrogation methods against terrorist suspects post-9/11. In particular, the government used waterboarding (pouring water over a cloth on the subject's face to simulate drowning), "walling" (slamming a subject into a false wall), forced standing in "stress positions," open-hand slaps, sensory deprivation, and confinement in a box that the captors said contained a deadly stinging insect, among other techniques. Some of this treatment was freely discussed, but some became public only when documents and photographs were released. In the years since these government actions became known, a significant body of literature has developed that documents and analyzes them.[28] For present purposes, I will focus on the legal questions raised by coercive interrogation.

In 1984, the international Convention against Torture (CAT) was signed. The CAT prohibits the use of torture by its signatories and defines torture as the infliction of severe physical or mental pain by (or with the consent of) a public official. The CAT also prohibits sending a person to another country where he or she will be tortured, and it bans cruel, inhuman, or degrading treatment (CIDT), which is treatment that falls short of torture. The ritual humiliation of prisoners at Abu Ghraib, where they were forced to stand naked and wear dog collars, is an example of CIDT (though U.S. officials would disagree). Significantly, the United States adopted the CAT with reservations. First, an act must be "specifically intended" to cause severe pain in order to constitute torture. This reservation would later be used by Bush administration lawyers to narrow the definition of torture and green-light a number of the techniques then in use. Second, CIDT would include only those practices already prohibited by the Fifth, Eighth, and Fourteenth Amendments to the Constitution.[29] In a perverse way, this reservation actually made the constitutional limits *less restrictive* than those of the international accord. And rhetorically, stating constitutional limits made the government appear to be acting lawfully. In practical fact, however, this reservation meant something quite different. It meant that the CIDT prohibition was superfluous, adding nothing new to existing law. If an act violated the Constitution's terms, it was already prohibited. The U.S. government was already constrained to follow those constitutional limits. But humiliation or degradation might not fall within due process or Eighth Amendment limits as those constitutional provisions were then construed. In that case, the interpretation of CIDT did not prohibit it.

Congress operationalized the CAT by enacting a criminal statute prohibiting torture. However, that statute contained the reservations detailed here and made no mention of CIDT.[30] The Bush administration seized on these openings in crafting an interrogation policy that constructed a putative legality while allowing the use of the techniques described earlier. In the infamous "Bybee memo" of 2002, administration lawyers construed severe pain as pain equivalent to "organ failure,"[31] citing a federal health care statute here in order to define severe pain in this way (the statute concerns emergency medical treatment). This argument was seen by many as a definitional stretch, to say the least, and in fact the administration backed away from it a few years later. In addition, the memo argued that "specific intent" referred only to torture practiced for its own sake. If infliction of severe pain is instrumental to another goal, such as interrogation, it does not count as torture. Finally, the memo proclaimed that the president's power to protect the nation rendered certain actions in pursuit of that goal—including torture—unreviewable by the courts.

The Supreme Court never ruled directly on the Bush administration's interrogation policies. The lower federal courts found procedural reasons to deny relief—as in the cases of Khalid El-Masri and Maher Arar, who were rendered to secret locations outside the United States, subjected to prolonged torture, and ultimately released when found to be innocent of any connection to terrorist groups. When President Obama took office in January 2009, he indicated that his administration would not utilize coercive interrogation techniques. He issued an executive order entitled "Ensuring Lawful Interrogations," which established the Geneva Conventions and the Army Field Manual as the legal standards for interrogation.[32] This step appeared to make a clean break with the policies of the previous administration. To the chagrin of some, Obama also indicated that he would not seek to prosecute any Bush administration officials for their involvement in coercive interrogation procedures, whether they had been advisers or participants. Despite this change in policy course, there is evidence that the Obama administration has sent some terror suspects to overseas locations for interrogation by other regimes.[33]

Redefining Due Process in the Context of Targeted Drone Strikes

The focus of controversy in Obama's antiterror policy is a different one: the targeted killing of terrorist suspects by drone aircraft strikes. The drone strikes against specific terrorist suspects became controversial for several reasons. They are different from other military operations because they are directed at named individuals rather than at enemy forces generally; the Israeli military has practiced this kind of targeted strike for many years. By using lethal force against a particular individual, the United States raises the question whether the strike is an assassination. Assassination is generally prohibited by the law of war and also violates a standing executive order. Moreover, the strikes have targeted U.S. citizens as well as foreign nationals. Anwar al-Awlaki, as U.S. citizen, was killed by a drone strike in Yemen in 2011.[34] Because the predator drones are operated remotely, the possibility for error is increased, and in fact civilian casualties have been frequent.

For many people, the most troubling aspect of the drone strike program is the asymmetry between the severity of its result and the paucity of its process. Arguably, targeting a person for killing is the most severe action a government can take, at least in terms of finality. Yet the procedural steps upon which a kill order is predicated are minimal. In 2013, the Obama administration released a white paper summarizing its legal justifications for using lethal force against suspected terrorists,[35] and the public learned that targets were selected by the president in consultation with his advisers. There was no formal finding of "guilt," no judicial approval given or sought. The administration said that each target could avoid attack by surrendering to U.S. forces and receiving a trial, but no one really expected that to happen.

The Obama administration justified the adequacy of its procedures by drawing a distinction between due process and judicial process. The Constitution requires that the government provide "due process of law" prior to depriving a person of life, liberty, or property. The rights of a criminal defendant to a hearing, to counsel, and to cross-examination of witnesses are components of due process in a criminal proceeding. The doctrine of due process as it has developed through Supreme Court decisions allows for some flexibility of application. In other words, the amount of process that is due depends on the type of deprivation the government seeks to accomplish. A criminal trial, a deportation, a forfeiture of property, and a denial of welfare benefits call for differing amounts of procedural protection. Citing this flexibility, the administration argued that due process did not always require *judicial* process—that is, due process could be satisfied in this context by nothing more than internal deliberations of the executive branch. Needless to say, this assertion went well beyond any existing conception of due process. It also requires an extraordinary level of trust in the executive on the part of the coordinate branches and the public because there is no mechanism of accountability or oversight for what are, quite literally, life-and-death decisions. Nor is there any way for the "targets" to contest their designation or to present exculpatory evidence.

The administration presented a number of arguments in support of targeted killings. In general, it noted that drone operations did not put the lives of U.S. military personnel at risk because the drones are unmanned. Additionally, targeted strikes could in theory reduce civilian casualties, since they are directed at particular individuals. The administration also emphasized that three conditions must be met before a lethal attack can be authorized: the individual (1) poses an imminent threat to the United States, (2) cannot be captured, and (3) will be attacked in accordance with the laws of war. For some commentators, the principal objection to the drone strike policy was not that enemy command and planning centers were being attacked but rather that the chosen procedures invest in the executive too much unreviewable discretion.

Conclusion

The war on terror implicates two components of the Magna Carta tradition: habeas corpus and due process. In assessing the state of the Magna Carta and common law constitutionalism during this period, it makes sense to consider each of these components in turn.

In view of the record of habeas litigation, one could ask what was accomplished by more than a decade of individual rights litigation on behalf of war on terror detainees. When the Supreme Court denied review of a group of habeas denials in 2012, it signaled to many observers that the Court was no longer committed to ensuring full and fair opportunities for review of detention at Guantanamo. Meanwhile, the D.C. Circuit continued to develop case law that was more favorable to the government than to petitioners, as the Supreme Court stayed out of the fray. Late in 2013, senior appeals judge Harry Edwards voiced his dissatisfaction with the developing habeas law of the D.C. Circuit in his concurring opinion in *Ali v. Obama*. That ruling affirmed denial of habeas relief by the district court. Edwards concurred because he was bound to follow the law of the circuit, but he expressed disagreement with it, noting that the outcome of the case would keep Ali detained for the duration of the war on terror—most likely the rest of his life. "It seems bizarre, to say the least,"

Edwards wrote, "that someone like Ali, who has never been charged with or found guilty of a criminal act and who has never 'planned, authorized, committed, or aided [any] terrorist attacks' is now marked for a life sentence." He continued, "The troubling question in these detainee cases is whether the law of the circuit has stretched the meaning of the AUMF [Authorization for Use of Military Force] and the NDAA [National Defense Authorization Act] so far beyond the terms of these statutory authorizations that habeas corpus proceedings like the one afforded Ali are functionally useless."[36] It is striking that someone directly involved with the detainee habeas process would make such a fundamental criticism of that process. So much effort and so many resources were expended in the effort to provide, in the words of the Court in *Boumediene*, a "meaningful opportunity" to contest detention, and yet the proceedings fell far short of that standard for many of the detainees. In a way, we have come full circle from 1215, when the English barons complained of unchecked executive power to detain and negotiated the Magna Carta in response.

One commentator, however, has urged a longer view of the efficacy of Guantanamo litigation. Steve Vladeck reminds us that the number of detainees has decreased dramatically, due in part to the determined efforts of human rights lawyers to pursue justice for them. In other words, the challenges to detention changed the government's practices and led them to release detainees even though there were few decisive legal victories. Additionally, as Vladeck points out, there were a number of habeas cases (fourteen, in fact) where the petitioner won and the government did not appeal. No appellate case law resulted, but those were successful actions nonetheless, and they made a concrete difference for the petitioners. Third, the courts were obliged to develop case law as a result of the detainee litigation, strengthening rule of law in an area cloaked in secrecy. These points are worth keeping in mind.[37]

One setback for a vigorous habeas procedure has been the development of case law that is overly solicitous of the concerns of the executive branch. Hearsay and coerced evidence are permitted. The government enjoys evidentiary presumptions of regularity even for evidence emerging out of the "fog of war." The preponderance of the evidence is enough to justify indefinite (and probably lifetime) detention. This case law is common law in the broadest sense, and yet it is not sensitive to the common law tradition. In fact, it rejects that tradition in its evidentiary and standard of proof principles. It is not guided by experience or practical reason so much as by concern for the functioning of the executive branch. Another way that the habeas law of the post-9/11 era diverges from the practice of common law constitutionalism is in its avoidance of extraterritoriality questions outside of Guantanamo. In his history of habeas corpus, Anthony Gregory has shown that the English monarchs sought to evade the reach of habeas corpus by transferring prisoners out of the realm—to Scotland, for example.[38] This abuse of executive power provoked complaint, too, from the North American colonists. The Bush administration followed the same practice when it seized and transferred prisoners to secret interrogation sites overseas. And as I discussed earlier, there is evidence that the Obama administration continued this practice. The D.C. Circuit has yet to apply the *Boumediene* holding—and habeas corpus—beyond Guantanamo to other extraterritorial sites. Thus, the war on terror has revived the practice of extraterritorial evasion of habeas, which was a scourge of liberty's advocates at common law.

It is unfortunate that the Supreme Court has declined to intervene in the D.C. Circuit's post-*Boumediene* development of habeas case law. Members of the Court had expressed concern about the government's view of habeas vis-à-vis war on terror detainees during oral argument in *Boumediene*. A number of themes emerged from the colloquy with Solicitor General Clement. The idea that there was nowhere for a detainee to make the argument that it was unlawful to detain him without charges for an indefinite period clearly troubled Justice Breyer. He asked, "If he cannot make that argument, how does this become an equivalent to habeas, since that happens to be the argument that a large number of these 305 people would like to make?"[39] Solicitor General Clement did not dispute that point. He conceded that such a challenge was not available to the detainees, but he justified his position by saying that the detainees were already getting far more process than they would have at common law. He used 1789 as the baseline and said that at that time a detainee would not have been entitled to the procedural protections the government was providing in 2008. In the oral argument of the *Boumediene* case, Clement argued,

> If the level of review provided by the DTA in the DTA petition were provided by statute in 1789 or even in 1941, for that matter, would it have been seen as a liberalization of the writ, or a contraction and suspension of the writ.
>
> And I think it is very, very clear that if this statute had passed, if this kind of review was provided in 1789 or in 1941, it would have been greeted as a remarkable—remarkable liberalization of the writ as it had then been understood.[40]

The problems with this argument were pointed out in rebuttal by petitioner's counsel, Seth Waxman. The CSRT proceedings were not more liberal. The government withheld information from detainees and their counsel in a "Kafkaesque" manner, such that they could not present an effective defense. Waxman cited the case of Murat Kurnaz, who was seized and detained on the accusation that he was associated with a terrorist who subsequently detonated a suicide bomb. At the CSRT, Kurnaz could not respond to this accusation because the government did not tell him the man's name. It was only when Kurnaz later obtained a lawyer (which CSRT respondents do not get) that his lawyer learned the name of the alleged terrorist and quickly proved that the man alleged to be a dead terrorist was not only alive but free of any terrorist association. The government had made a mistake. Waxman's point was that the fundamentally unfair CSRT proceedings were not more "liberal" than earlier forms of detention review used in 1789 or 1941 but in fact clearly worse.[41]

Moreover, Guantanamo detainees were being treated differently than they would have been in 1789 in other ways as well: subject to indefinite detention and categorized simultaneously as "not-prisoners of war" and "not-criminal defendants." At oral argument the Court seized on this point and criticized the government for trying to have it both ways: saying that the writ of habeas corpus was unavailable to prisoners of war at common law but also denying that the detainees were prisoners of war. Justice Ginsberg found this argument to be inconsistent.[42]

Also, the question of whether the writ of habeas corpus had actually been suspended by Congress loomed large in *Boumediene*. It had also troubled the Court two years earlier in *Hamdan v. Rumsfeld*, where Solicitor General Clement seemed to suggest that Congress could suspend the writ implicitly, or inadvertently. Justice Souter was troubled by that suggestion. "Isn't there a pretty good argument," he asked "that a suspension of the writ of congress is just about the most stupendously significant act that the congress of the United States can take? And, therefore, we ought to be at least a little slow to accept your argument that it can be done from pure inadvertence?"[43] Without a clear statement from Congress, Souter was unwilling to infer that suspension had occurred.

Clearly, these concerns troubled the Court and led to its holding requiring habeas rights for the detainees. Thus, the Court was able to apply common law principles to the constitutional question in *Boumediene* in a way that drew on experience and present context. But when it left the lower courts to develop case law without further input, its earlier concerns about meaningful habeas review went unheeded, and the opportunity to make habeas effective for 9/11 detainees was lost.

So much for habeas corpus. Due process has also suffered during the war on terror. The Obama administration moved away from coercive interrogation, which was a positive step to take, but it has developed the practice of targeted lethal strikes against individual terror suspects. This practice is supported in legal terms by a novel and troubling conception of due process. The argument that due process can be provided without *judicial* process (i.e., without a hearing) has been forcefully asserted by administration lawyers. This claim flies in the face of existing due process jurisprudence. It is true that the Supreme Court has said due process is a flexible concept, but to remove the hearing requirement from due process simply stretches it too far, especially when the end result extinguishes a human life. When we recall that "due process" originated in the "law of the land" provision of Article 39 of the Magna Carta, the deficiency of a due process proceeding without a hearing stands out quite sharply. The administration argued that a high-level executive branch official could make the unilateral determination to use lethal force against an individual. If the original purpose of the Magna Carta's Article 39 was to restrain executive power by the rule of law, it is difficult to imagine a more direct repudiation of that purpose than the targeted killing program, which makes lethal force lawful if launched by an internal executive deliberation.

David Luban has suggested that the response to 9/11 has generated a "torture culture," which results from the accommodation of torture practices within liberal ideology. Torture for "victor's pleasure," for intimidation, for punishment, or even for extracting criminal confessions cannot be reconciled with a political culture that abhors cruelty, values individual rights, and fears state power. However, use of torture to prevent mass casualties *can* be accommodated. In fact, this problematic itself (the rights of the one versus the well-being of the many) draws together the "two great Western traditions of deontological and utilitarian ethics."[44] Torture can be accommodated this way, Luban argues, because the state is not being cruel or wanton but rather is seeking to maximize social well-being by averting catastrophe.[45] This ideology first started to take hold after 9/11 when an angry and frightened public began to flirt with the idea of torture. It became entrenched when the Bush administration engaged legal specialists in the project of manipulating doctrine in order to produce legal rationales for torture and CIDT. Push-back and resistance to the torture culture have come from civil society: from human rights groups, public intellectuals, and alternative media. But it has also come, at times, from the courts. Perceiving their role as a bulwark against unprincipled and excessive executive power, federal district courts and the Supreme Court in *Hamdi, Hamdan, Rasul*, and *Boumediene* have apprehended the core importance of safeguarding individual liberty by preserving habeas corpus. At those moments, the courts reflected the orientation of common law constitutionalism with its attentiveness to tradition and its flexibility to respond to new legal contexts.

To be sure, legal actors are not always practicing common law constitutionalism when they look to the past for guidance. It is an inevitable and indelible feature of our legal system that each side in a dispute will construct a narrative of past legal development that favors its side in the dispute. This is evident in *Hamdan* and *Boumediene* as the government cites English practice to support its denial of the writ, while petitioners' counsel cites the same history but reads it differently. It is difficult to find methodological consistency in the words of advocates, who are, by necessity, result-oriented. The statements of courts are easier to evaluate. In the case of post-9/11 rulings, there are instances, such as those cited earlier, where courts acted to restrain state power by enforcing time-honored forms of legal challenge. At other times, such as the ongoing development of executive-friendly habeas case law by the D.C. Circuit, courts' actions clearly show a solicitude for the institutional impulses of the executive (the executive's need to act quickly, to conduct foreign policy freely, to err on the side of denying rights). At such times, the courts' actions can be seen as a step backward. Speaking most broadly, common law constitutionalism is an approach to constitutional interpretation that looks to tradition and precedent to give meaning to constitutional concepts. However, in the post-9/11 period, as in other periods, tradition and precedent do not suggest the same answers to everyone. During the period preceding *Erie v. Tompkins*, the federal courts relied on tradition to guide constitutional interpretation, and the result was favorable to the interests of business corporations and unfavorable to individuals such as workers and tort victims. Similarly, the courts (and government lawyers) involved in detainee cases post-9/11 used tradition to support restrictive interpretations of detainees' rights. Is there a way to argue for a principled use of tradition and precedent in constitutional disputes concerning individual liberty? In other words, what would a normative defense of common law constitutionalism look like? That is the question to be taken up next, in the conclusion.

8

Conclusion

In the preceding chapters, I have documented and analyzed references to the Magna Carta during various periods in U.S. legal history. Sometimes those references were explicit, mentioning the document by name, and at other times the allusions to it were indirect and phrased in terms of the "rights of Englishmen," the heritage of liberty, and the like. In the colonies, the language of the Magna Carta's Article 39 was replicated in colonial charters, and when independence came, the Constitution took on Magna Carta provisions in the suspension clause and the Jury Trial and Due Process Clauses of the Bill of Rights. In the pre–Civil War years, debates over slavery made reference to the Magna Carta—particularly with regard to the capture, detention, and return of fugitive slaves. During the early twentieth century, the rise and fall of the federal common law implicated the Magna Carta as the perception of common law changed from a body of revealed truths to law generated by a sovereign. And in the Warren years, the Court frequently cited common law liberties (as well as the Magna Carta by name) as it expanded conceptions of individual rights in constitutional law. The Rehnquist Court took up questions of habeas corpus but moved doctrine in the opposite direction, curtailing the reach and availability of the writ. And after

9/11, the Bush and Obama administrations' waging of the war on terror led the Supreme Court to invoke the Magna Carta as the Court confronted executive detention practices. Recalling this history serves to make a *descriptive* point: that the Magna Carta has influenced U.S. legal development as the Supreme Court has generated individual rights doctrine through case law. It is important to see the role of the Magna Carta in that process—and that its influence has extended into our time.

Normative Defense of Common Law Constitutionalism: The Living Constitution

I have also argued normatively, though, in *defense* of the Court's reliance on the Magna Carta over time. The continued invocation of a document that is not formally part of our laws (though the Constitution makes reference to it) is valid and appropriate. It is a part of an approach to constitutional interpretation that has functioned well to protect individual liberty.

In *The Living Constitution*, David Strauss notes the indeterminacy of the constitutional text at numerous points. Like Akhil Amar, Strauss concludes when faced with this indeterminacy that it is necessary at those points to look outside the text for guidance in interpreting and applying its provisions. Like Amar, he cites examples where the text alone simply does not tell us enough to allow resolution of a constitutional dispute. Whereas Amar notes the absurdity of a literal reading of certain provisions (e.g., allowing the vice president to preside over his own impeachment trial), Strauss observes that key questions go unanswered if we are limited to the literal meaning of the text, as when the First Amendment says that "Congress shall make no law" abridging freedom of speech. We know that some speech will *not* be protected, such as "scream[ing] in the ear of a cardiac patient,"[1] but how do we know what counts and what does not? The text alone cannot always tell us. More than Amar, though, Strauss emphasizes the role of judicial discretion and individual judgment in rendering decisions where extratextual guidance is needed.

Strauss explains the development of constitutional doctrine as a necessarily open and contingent endeavor. It is not just that the "living constitution" approach is superior to the originalist alternative; developing the text as a living document is what the Supreme Court was *actually doing* when it shaped certain basic doctrines. Here is Strauss describing the law of free speech: "It developed over time, fitfully, by a process in which principles and standards were tried and sometimes eventually accepted, sometimes abandoned, sometimes modified, in light of experience and an ongoing, explicit assessment of whether they were sound as a matter of policy. The law of the First Amendment is a creation of the living Constitution."[2] As the passage shows, this conception of how the justices go about their work leaves much to their discretion. Common law constitutionalism allows them the space to develop doctrine by applying precedent critically. The same conception is evident in Strauss's description of equal protection jurisprudence at the midpoint of the twentieth century: "In concluding that separate could never be equal, the Court in Brown was taking one further step in a well-established progression. It was acting not as the interpreter of the views of mid-nineteenth-century politicians, but as a court with the responsibility for the evolution—in a properly restrained, common law fashion—of the living Constitution."[3]

Critics of the "living constitution" approach, or common law constitutionalism, charge that it allows judges to do what they want, to assign whatever meanings they choose to the text they are called upon to interpret. This criticism is misguided. It sets up a false dichotomy between a method constrained by a clear "right answer" on the one hand and a standardless, arbitrary choice on the other. As I have said, the opposite methodological pole to the living constitution approach is originalism. The originalist critique of the living constitution usually proceeds from the assumption stated earlier: that in absence of originalism, judges are free to choose and apply any meaning they want. But this assumption relies in turn on a tacit belief in the existence of a right answer. It suggests that an objectively correct, verifiable, and measurable understanding of constitutional provisions can be found, and that everything but that right answer is demonstrably wrong and false. In fact, however, things are not so clear or simple in either direction. In many cases, originalism itself does not dictate an answer either but rather involves a choice. These choices arise when the evidence of the drafters' intent or accepted meaning is ambiguous. They also arise when original understanding would yield an absurd result. In these instances, the judge who claims to adhere to originalism chooses the alternative that seems superior and in doing so looks to something other than originalism. The discussion of legal formalism in chapter 4 showed how seemingly objective and correct legal decisions often masked policy preferences and interests with a rhetoric of discovered truth. This insight continues to apply with force today.

There is reason to dispute the other side of the dichotomy as well. Nonoriginalist judges *are*, in fact, constrained in their decisional choices, but in a less obvious way than critics suppose. Arbitrary, sloppy, or nakedly partisan decisions risk incurring legitimacy costs for the Court as an institution. While it is possible in the short term for the Court to make that kind of decision, it will exact costs over time as *Lochner v. New York* and *Dred Scott v. Sandford* did. Mistakes are observable even without a "right answer" of the originalist variety against which to measure them, and they lead to criticisms of the Court. Moreover, even originalists can behave in ways that risk legitimacy, as did the Rehnquist Court when it decided *Bush v. Gore*, setting aside its typical jurisprudential assumptions and awarding the presidency to a conservative Republican. Many people saw the *Bush v. Gore* decision as overtly partisan, and because of it they questioned the legitimacy of the Court for years afterward.

Finally, there is a more subtle measurement of when the Court has made a good (and, in a sense, "right" decision). Strauss notes that certain cases such as *Brown v. Board of Education* came to be seen as correct by virtually everyone, even though they were criticized when first handed down. And *Brown* was correct even though it was not supported by the Fourteenth Amendment's original meaning. It was right in a broader and more subtle way. The principles that guided the Court to decide *Brown* as it did—a basic notion of equality, a compelling claim to justice, and a whittling away of the misguided precedent stated by *Plessy*—pointed to an answer and called for wisdom and flexibility. The Court had indeed been "free" to decide the case differently, but it applied those principles in a way that led it to a ruling that has gained support across the full spectrum of public opinion, of legal specialists and laypeople alike, in the sixty years since it was rendered.

In its rejection of a pre-given "right answer" to fundamental questions, common law constitutionalism invites a comparison to existentialist philosophy. The existentialists believed that their rejection of universal moral standards placed a great responsibility on individual moral agents themselves. They alone were responsible for their choices, and this was both freeing and terrifying because they could not displace blame or consequences onto a belief system, social norm, or community judgment. Their freedom to define themselves through their own individual existence came at a price. A judge who grapples with precedent, examines tradition, and ultimately decides what to accept or modify or reject confronts a similarly daunting moment each time a decision is called for. There is no pre-given answer to rely on that is guaranteed to be correct. Precedent and tradition must be considered because ignoring them risks repeating earlier mistakes.[4] But there are times when precedent must yield to what

Holmes called "the felt necessities of the time," and judges must make that choice between continuity and change throughout their time on the bench.

Originalism has been championed most strongly in recent years by conservative jurists and commentators such as Robert Bork, William Rehnquist, and (in his own "original meaning" version) Antonin Scalia. But it is not necessarily or exclusively oriented this way. Recall that Justice Hugo Black's influential arguments from original intent helped to advance individual rights during the Warren years, and Black's writing on incorporation of the Bill of Rights proved to be an influential contribution to constitutional law. In a recent essay, Amar argues that originalism need not be the province of conservatives alone.[5] This insight reminds us to keep methodology and ideology distinct. An interpretive approach can be put to use for more than one end. Nonetheless, the objections to originalism as a theory apply with force even when the theory is decoupled from an antilibertarian perspective.

Epistemology, Tradition, and Right Answers

The relationship among the common law, innovation, and the rights of individuals has not been fixed or stable. In the late nineteenth century, federal courts claimed to be authoritative in interpreting the common law, and this meant that they could say with certainty what it meant. The "true" meaning of law was something that lay waiting to be discovered by those competent to unearth it. More often than not, those discovered principles led to decisions favoring powerful actors in society, particularly the developing industrial interests. The federal courts perceived their role as facilitating the growth of industry: that was the way to move society forward. Following the common law meant adherence to tradition.

With the growth of pragmatism and the openness to social science methods and data brought on by Legal Realism, common law interpretation in the twentieth century was reoriented once again. Justice Holmes urged that law was not some "outside thing," but rather a process of correction through experience. Holmes did not embrace all of what the Realists proposed, but he did think that law should be responsive to changing conditions, and he urged its interpreters to adopt a critical attitude toward tradition. For mid-twentieth-century justices, this critical attitude sometimes led them to break with tradition, to abandon or modify precedent. It might seem inconsistent, at first glance, to say that common law constitutionalism relies on tradition in developing legal meaning but also rejects tradition at times. In fact, however, there is no contradiction in saying that tradition and judgment both guide legal interpretation. Thus, Strauss can say that "under a common law approach, the long-standing nature of . . . traditions supports the legitimacy of establishing a constitutional right."[6] And he can also defend the jurisprudence in the free speech and equal protection areas that modified precedent in response to new challenges posed by a changing society. In common law constitutionalism the role of tradition is strong, but it is nuanced.

Habeas Corpus at Common Law, Habeas Corpus Today

Habeas commentators have often compared the procedures used at common law to habeas proceedings today, noting that contemporary petitioners ask for more than was required in the past. We have seen this comparison in the oral arguments in the detainee cases, in Judge Friendly's article on innocence and postconviction relief, and in Anthony Gregory's description of habeas actions (though Gregory takes a more critical stance toward it). The commentators note that at common law the return (the state's answer to the petition) satisfied the habeas process when the government stated in its response that the prisoner was being held pursuant to a valid conviction or other lawful authorization. That avowal was enough to assure the court that detention was not contrary to law, and it brought the proceeding to an end. In each of the previously mentioned contexts where this principle was invoked, the writer suggested that this limitation precluded the kind of searching habeas review that petitioners urge today (though Gregory sees this outcome as undesirable). Judge Friendly asserted that Justice Brennan got the history wrong in *Fay v. Noia* and that English courts were far more limited and deferential to state power than Brennan suggests. Solicitor General Clement suggested that Guantanamo detainees seeking habeas review were vastly overreaching by asking for the courts to undertake substantive review of the circumstances of their confinement because earlier courts would not have questioned those circumstances once the government had affirmed that the detainees were enemy combatants. And Gregory noted that in the fugitive slave cases the same problem arose: once the government responded to a habeas petition by saying that a person was detained pursuant to the Fugitive Slave Law, the court was powerless to grant relief. Two points deserve emphasis here. First, there is a complexity to the concept of habeas corpus that must be acknowledged. We tend to think of the mere availability of habeas corpus as a sufficient protection against unjust or illegal confinement. But we need to know more about what is happening at the implementation level in order to determine how well that safeguard actually works. Consider the fugitive slave disputes. When a detainee challenged his detention in custody of a federal marshal by filing a habeas petition in state court, the state court judge would require a return by the government showing lawful detention. In response, the federal marshal would cite the Fugitive Slave Law, and the habeas petition would be defeated. Similarly, if the government responded to a habeas petition by saying that the prisoner was being held for treason, the inquiry would be at an end. In short, the effectiveness of habeas cannot be judged apart from these details of implementation.

The second point is related to the first, and it has to do with innovation and habeas law. If tradition is inviolable, then courts today should not alter in any way the details of habeas proceedings as they occurred in seventeenth- and eighteenth-century English courts. But I have argued in this book that common law constitutionalism does not always require adherence to tradition even though tradition is often its guide. A critical and reflective consideration of what courts have done in the past allows judges interpreting the U.S. Constitution to draw on experience and tradition while always seeking a closer approximation of the justice to which earlier common law courts aspired. The fundamental problem of avoiding punishment of the innocent—which is, after all, a core part of the concept of habeas corpus as it develops through the Magna Carta tradition—has occupied judges for centuries. We know that innocent people are tried, convicted, and executed today, and so judges must continue to struggle with the problem. DNA testing is helpful in this regard, but as we know from the *Osborne* case discussed in chapter 6, disputes continue to arise over the use of DNA. The Supreme Court should constitutionalize the issue of access to DNA testing, but it declined to do so in *Osborne*.

Due Process through the Common Law Lens

A number of Supreme Court opinions through the years have noted that due process is traceable to the "law of the land" phrase in the Magna Carta's Article 39. This linkage signifies to many commentators that the Magna Carta declared a fundamental principle of liberty that guided English and American courts as they decided individual rights disputes. Developments in the interpretation of due process have broadened its application while maintaining the deep connection to Magna Carta. The differentiation of substantive and procedural due process discussed at several points in this book is one example of that development, which has come about for the most part through the use of common law constitutionalism. A form of due process was used to ground the Court's 2003 decision in *Lawrence v. Texas*,[7] which recognized the right to privacy in intimate same-sex relationships. The decision relied on substantive due process to say that "personhood" is an integral part of liberty, and that choosing one's associations (including intimate relationships) is part of developing one's personhood. This was a modification of the previous understanding of due process, but it did not arise out of nowhere. Rather, it extended the thinking of Warren and Burger Court privacy decisions. The same thing had occurred half a century earlier, when the Court used substantive due process to distance the modern conception of liberty from tortures allowed earlier in English history. *Rochin v. California*[8] outlawed stomach pumping as a method of obtaining evidence in a drug-related case, finding that method "too close to the rack and the screw."

As a method of interpretation, common law constitutionalism can lead its practitioners to different results. There is no guarantee that a particular opinion purporting to rely on the method will become settled and lasting precedent that gains widespread and long-standing acceptance. If critical judgment is one of the hallmarks of common law constitutionalism, then we should subject the resulting decisions to critical scrutiny in order to test how well the method has worked to yield good case law.

The 1884 case of *Hurtado v. California*[9] is worth examining to see common law constitutionalism in operation. In a sense, *Hurtado* is an anomaly because it uses common law constitutionalism and reaches a pro–law enforcement, antidefendant result. Nonetheless, it serves to illustrate how discretion can lead to an ill-advised result—not because it goes against the defendant but because its logic leads to a dangerous view of legislative authority that had already been confronted and rejected in England.

Hurtado was a Supreme Court decision that went against the petitioner, who was a death row inmate. The opinion has been cited widely for its extensive discussion of the Magna Carta's influence on U.S. constitutional law. It was a criminal procedure case where due process in pretrial proceedings was at issue. Hurtado had been convicted of murder and sentenced to death, and he claimed that his due process rights were violated when the prosecution used an "information" rather than a grand jury proceeding to determine whether there was sufficient evidence to charge him with the crime.

A grand jury is a closed and secret proceeding in which jurors hear evidence and decide whether or not to indict one or more suspects. If the jurors hand down an indictment, the case can proceed to trial; if not, it must be dismissed. Because the grand jury meets in secret, the suspects are shielded from public exposure, and if the evidence is insufficient to indict, they go free without notoriety. The grand jury also functions as a screening mechanism ensuring that only cases that meet a certain evidentiary threshold will proceed to trial. An "information," by contrast, is a statement of charges. The information can be filed after a preliminary hearing, which is an alternative form of determining whether a case should proceed to trial. However, a preliminary hearing is not always used prior to the filing of an information. A case that proceeds to trial based simply on an information rather than a grand jury verdict has not had its evidence tested in the same way. In recognition of this difference, the Fifth Amendment requires that "no person shall be held to answer for a capital, or otherwise infamous crime, unless on a presentment or indictment of a Grand Jury." In 1884, this provision was not applied against the states, so that the grand jury requirement was mandatory only for federal prosecutions.

Hurtado argued that due process required a grand jury indictment in a capital case like his, and the question for the Court was whether due process in state court proceedings did in fact include a grand jury. The majority analyzed the question by starting with the Magna Carta and then looking to commentary on it by Coke, Blackstone, and others. They summarized the construction urged by the defendant as follows: "By immemorial usage it has acquired a fixed, definite, and technical meaning . . . and which, having been the birthright and inheritance of every English subject, crossed the Atlantic with the colonists it has now been added as an additional security to the individual against oppression by the States themselves."[10] Thus, from the petitioner's point of view, the grand jury was "an essential part of due process of law, in order that he may not be harassed or destroyed by prosecutions founded only upon private malice or popular fury."[11]

But the Court saw things differently. They wanted to say that the meaning of due process changed over time. The majority explained that "to hold that such a characteristic is essential to due process of law, would be to deny every quality of the law but its age, and to render it incapable of progress or improvement. It would be to stamp upon our jurisprudence the unchangeableness attributed to the laws of the Medes and Persians."[12] The Court insisted that, "owing to the progressive development of legal ideas and institutions in England, the words of Magna Charta stood for very different things at the time of the separation of the American colonies from what they represented originally."[13] They also offered that "this flexibility and capacity for growth and adaptation is the peculiar boast and excellence of the common law."[14]

This is an argument that tradition must sometimes yield to innovation, and in making the argument, the Court essentially read the Magna Carta against itself: "There is nothing in Magna Charta, rightly construed as a broad charter of public right and law, which ought to exclude the best ideas of all systems and of every age; and as it was the characteristic principle of the common law to draw its inspiration from every fountain of justice, we are not to assume that the sources of its supply have been exhausted."[15] This passage emphasizes the aspect of common law constitutionalism that calls for critical, flexible interpretation of foundational texts. It so happens that the method yields, here, a pro-government rather than a pro–individual rights result. The Magna Carta was a document created to limit the power of the government. Does that mean that it cannot support a pro-government result in any case? That is a difficult question, but the Court's next argumentative move makes it unnecessary to answer because the Court certainly takes things too far: "It follows that any legal proceeding enforced by public authority, whether sanctioned by age and custom, or newly devised in the discretion of the legislative power, in furtherance of the general public good, which regards and preserves these principles of liberty and justice, must be held to be due process of law."[16]

Anything the legislature enacts, the majority says here, amounts to due process. Thus, the due process guarantee originating in the Magna Carta and fixed in the Bill of Rights is powerless to challenge state power when deployed by the legislature; only the executive (presumably) is constrained by due process. This restrictive reading ignores English history (recall disputes over parliamentary supremacy cited in chapter 1), and it renders a core concept of constitutional law ineffective.

Hurtado has been cited frequently through the years for its many statements about the Magna Carta. And some states now use preliminary hearings (which even have some advantages for defendants) in place of grand juries. Today, the dicta in *Hurtado* cited earlier strike the modern reader as extravagant and anachronistic. *Hurtado* shows that tradition and innovation can be approached in different ways (to pro-government as well as pro-individual ends). And even though *Hurtado* was not overruled, its statements regarding the source of due process and the extent of due process rights diminished in significance as constitutional doctrine developed in the next century.

A Living Constitution for the Future

Some questions recur in the life of the law, and some answers are similar to those provided in the past. Strauss describes the arguments made by the originalists in our time, and among them he notes "moderate originalism": a variety of originalism in which "what is binding is not the specific original understandings but instead the principles that the framers or the ratifiers of the Constitution were understood to be establishing."[17] This originalism one step removed recalls an earlier interpretive orientation detailed in chapter 3: the radical branch of antislavery constitutionalism. Some abolitionists wanted to argue that the Constitution prohibited slavery, but they were faced with the obvious problem of explicit constitutional references to slavery that recognized its existence. So they argued that the Constitution was antislavery *in its essence*. Notwithstanding specific references to the contrary, there was a deep pro-liberty norm, these abolitionists argued, that gave life and force to the U.S. Constitution. The problem with both of these arguments (the older and newer forms), as Strauss points out, is that they operate at a level of generality where they prove little or nothing. Arguments about textual meaning that are abstracted from textual evidence are unpersuasive. In truth, these are arguments for a living constitution, albeit in disguised form.

After detailing the ways in which it has produced important and laudable Supreme Court decisions, Strauss sums up the attributes of common law constitutionalism: "intellectual humility, a sense of the complexity of the problems faced by our society, a respect for the accumulated wisdom of the past, and a willingness to rethink when necessary and when consistent with those virtues."[18] This formulation encapsulates the approach to judicial decision making that treats the Constitution as a living document. It also describes what Supreme Court justices do in a way that many of them encountered in this book would approve, from Curtis to Holmes to Brandeis to Douglas to Frankfurter to Brennan. Those jurists, intellectually and temperamentally diverse and separated temporally across two centuries, made important contributions to constitutional law by approaching it as Strauss describes, and although they often criticized each other freely, their legacy can be said to share the common elements listed earlier.

Where does the Magna Carta fit within this description? It is a written document "under glass," as Strauss says of the U.S. Constitution, and it was duly executed and successively renewed. Its terms specify limitations on government power. In all of these ways, the Magna Carta resembles the U.S. Constitution. But it originated in a governmental system that never had a written constitution, so it has retained a fundamental importance as a symbol of individual liberty. In the American colonies it was cited as a source of rights claims before the federal constitution existed, and it was embodied in the constitutional text by reference to habeas corpus in Article I and due process (law of the land) in the Bill of Rights. The Magna Carta generated an unwritten rights tradition, and the U.S. Constitution generated common law constitutionalism. The general idea of restraining the government from acting against individuals has produced specific procedural protections (due process rights) and a form of action (habeas corpus) that have proved effective over 800 years, though not perfectly so. Those protections have in turn been honored and refined by judges seeking to apply the law to recurring problems in changing contexts. It is difficult to think about the Magna Carta apart from common law constitutionalism, since that interpretive tradition has kept the Magna Carta relevant and vital right through the present era of global terrorism and modern detention practices. At the same time, it is hard to imagine common law constitutionalism without the Magna Carta. The core concept of the Great Charter—restraining the executive by the rule of law—has been the most basic aspiration of modern political orders, and they have drawn support and inspiration from the Magna Carta for centuries. As judges look to tradition and precedent in flexible, critical, and pragmatic ways, seeking to adapt and utilize what works, they have turned to the Magna Carta in 1815, 1856, 1963, and 2008. The Magna Carta has helped to structure and organize a discourse of liberty in U.S. courts, and the courts can and should further that discourse into the future.

Appendix

The Magna Carta, 1215

JOHN, by the grace of God King of England, Lord of Ireland, Duke of Normandy and Aquitaine, and Count of Anjou, to his archbishops, bishops, abbots, earls, barons, justices, foresters, sheriffs, stewards, servants, and to all his officials and loyal subjects, Greeting.

KNOW THAT BEFORE GOD, for the health of our soul and those of our ancestors and heirs, to the honour of God, the exaltation of the holy Church, and the better ordering of our kingdom, at the advice of our reverend fathers Stephen, archbishop of Canterbury, primate of all England, and cardinal of the holy Roman Church, Henry archbishop of Dublin, William bishop of London, Peter bishop of Winchester, Jocelin bishop of Bath and Glastonbury, Hugh bishop of Lincoln, Walter bishop of Worcester, William bishop of Coventry, Benedict bishop of Rochester, Master Pandulf subdeacon and member of the papal household, Brother Aymeric master of the knighthood of the Temple in England, William Marshal earl of Pembroke, William earl of Salisbury, William earl of Warren, William earl of Arundel, Alan de Galloway constable of Scotland, Warin Fitz Gerald, Peter Fitz Herbert, Hubert de Burgh seneschal of Poitou, Hugh de Neville, Matthew Fitz Herbert, Thomas Basset, Alan Basset, Philip Daubeny, Robert de Roppeley, John Marshal, John Fitz Hugh, and other loyal subjects:

(1) FIRST, THAT WE HAVE GRANTED TO GOD, and by this present charter have confirmed for us and our heirs in perpetuity, that the English Church shall be free, and shall have its rights undiminished, and its liberties unimpaired. That we wish this so to be observed, appears from the fact that of our own free will, before the outbreak of the present dispute between us and our barons, we granted and confirmed by charter the freedom of the Church's elections—a right reckoned to be of the greatest necessity and importance to it—and caused this to be confirmed by Pope Innocent III. This freedom we shall observe ourselves, and desire to be observed in good faith by our heirs in perpetuity.

TO ALL FREE MEN OF OUR KINGDOM we have also granted, for us and our heirs for ever, all the liberties written out below, to have and to keep for them and their heirs, of us and our heirs:

(2) If any earl, baron, or other person that holds lands directly of the Crown, for military service, shall die, and at his death his heir shall be of full age and owe a "relief," the heir shall have his inheritance on payment of the ancient scale of "relief." That is to say, the heir or heirs of an earl shall pay £100 for the entire earl's barony, the heir or heirs of a knight 100s. at most for the entire knight's "fee," and any man that owes less shall pay less, in accordance with the ancient usage of "fees."

(3) But if the heir of such a person is under age and a ward, when he comes of age he shall have his inheritance without "relief" or fine.

(4) The guardian of the land of an heir who is under age shall take from it only reasonable revenues, customary dues, and feudal services. He shall do this without destruction or damage to men or property. If we have given the guardianship of the land to a sheriff, or to any person answerable to us for the revenues, and he commits destruction or damage, we will exact compensation from him, and the land shall be entrusted to two worthy and prudent men of the same "fee," who shall be answerable to us for the revenues, or to the person to whom we have assigned them. If we have given or sold to anyone the guardianship of such land, and he causes destruction or damage, he shall lose the guardianship of it, and it shall be handed over to two worthy and prudent men of the same "fee," who shall be similarly answerable to us.

(5) For so long as a guardian has guardianship of such land, he shall maintain the houses, parks, fish preserves, ponds, mills, and everything else pertaining to it, from the revenues of the land itself. When the heir comes of age, he shall restore the whole land to him, stocked with plough teams and such implements of husbandry as the season demands and the revenues from the land can reasonably bear.

(6) Heirs may be given in marriage, but not to someone of lower social standing. Before a marriage takes place, it shall be made known to the heir's next-of-kin.

(7) At her husband's death, a widow may have her marriage portion and inheritance at once and without trouble. She shall pay nothing for her dower, marriage portion, or any inheritance that she and her husband held jointly on the day of his death. She may remain in her husband's house for forty days after his death, and within this period her dower shall be assigned to her.

(8) No widow shall be compelled to marry, so long as she wishes to remain without a husband. But she must give security that she will not marry without royal consent, if she holds her lands of the Crown, or without the consent of whatever other lord she may hold them of.

(9) Neither we nor our officials will seize any land or rent in payment of a debt, so long as the debtor has movable goods sufficient to discharge the debt. A debtor's sureties shall not be distrained upon so long as the debtor himself can discharge his debt. If, for lack of means, the debtor is unable to discharge his debt, his sureties shall be answerable for it. If they so desire, they may have the debtor's lands and rents until they have received satisfaction for the debt that they paid for him, unless the debtor can show that he has settled his obligations to them.

(10) If anyone who has borrowed a sum of money from Jews dies before the debt has been repaid, his heir shall pay no interest on the debt for so long as he remains under age, irrespective of whom he holds his lands. If such a debt falls into the hands of the Crown, it will take nothing except the principal sum specified in the bond.

(11) If a man dies owing money to Jews, his wife may have her dower and pay nothing towards the debt from it. If he leaves children that are under age, their needs may also be provided for on a scale appropriate to the size of his holding of lands. The debt is to be paid out of the residue, reserving the service due to his feudal lords. Debts owed to persons other than Jews are to be dealt with similarly.

(12) No "scutage" or "aid" may be levied in our kingdom without its general consent, unless it is for the ransom of our person, to make our eldest son a knight, and (once) to marry our eldest daughter. For these purposes only a reasonable "aid" may be levied. "Aids" from the city of London are to be treated similarly.

(13) The city of London shall enjoy all its ancient liberties and free customs, both by land and by water. We also will and grant that all other cities, boroughs, towns, and ports shall enjoy all their liberties and free customs.

(14) To obtain the general consent of the realm for the assessment of an "aid"—except in the three cases specified above—or a "scutage," we will cause the archbishops, bishops, abbots, earls, and greater barons to be summoned individually by letter. To those who hold lands directly of us we will cause a general summons to be issued, through the sheriffs and other officials, to come together on a fixed day (of which at least forty days notice shall be given) and at a fixed place. In all letters of summons, the cause of the summons will be stated. When a summons has been issued, the business appointed for the day shall go forward in accordance with the resolution of those present, even if not all those who were summoned have appeared.

(15) In future we will allow no one to levy an "aid" from his free men, except to ransom his person, to make his eldest son a knight, and (once) to marry his eldest daughter. For these purposes only a reasonable "aid" may be levied.

(16) No man shall be forced to perform more service for a knight's "fee," or other free holding of land, than is due from it.

(17) Ordinary lawsuits shall not follow the royal court around, but shall be held in a fixed place.

(18) Inquests of *novel disseisin*, *mort d'ancestor*, and *darrein presentment* shall be taken only in their proper county court. We ourselves, or in our absence abroad our chief justice, will send two justices to each county four times a year, and these justices, with four knights of the county elected by the county itself, shall hold the assizes in the county court, on the day and in the place where the court meets.

(19) If any assizes cannot be taken on the day of the county court, as many knights and freeholders shall afterwards remain behind, of those who have attended the court, as will suffice for the administration of justice, having regard to the volume of business to be done.

(20) For a trivial offence, a free man shall be fined only in proportion to the degree of his offence, and for a serious offence correspondingly, but not so heavily as to deprive him of his livelihood. In the same way, a merchant shall be spared his merchandise, and a husbandman the implements of his husbandry, if they fall upon the mercy of a royal court. None of these fines shall be imposed except by the assessment on oath of reputable men of the neighbourhood.

(21) Earls and barons shall be fined only by their equals, and in proportion to the gravity of their offence.

(22) A fine imposed upon the lay property of a clerk in holy orders shall be assessed upon the same principles, without reference to the value of his ecclesiastical benefice.

(23) No town or person shall be forced to build bridges over rivers except those with an ancient obligation to do so.

(24) No sheriff, constable, coroners, or other royal officials are to hold lawsuits that should be held by the royal justices.

(25) Every county, hundred, wapentake, and tithing shall remain at its ancient rent, without increase, except the royal demesne manors.

(26) If at the death of a man who holds a lay "fee" of the Crown, a sheriff or royal official produces royal letters patent of summons for a debt due to the Crown, it shall be lawful for them to seize and list movable goods found in the lay "fee" of the dead man to the value of the debt, as assessed by worthy men. Nothing shall be removed until the whole debt is paid, when the residue shall be given over to the executors to carry out the dead man's will. If no debt is due to the Crown, all the movable goods shall be regarded as the property of the dead man, except the reasonable shares of his wife and children.

(27) If a free man dies intestate, his movable goods are to be distributed by his next-of-kin and friends, under the supervision of the Church. The rights of his debtors are to be preserved.

(28) No constable or other royal official shall take corn or other movable goods from any man without immediate payment, unless the seller voluntarily offers postponement of this.

(29) No constable may compel a knight to pay money for castle-guard if the knight is willing to undertake the guard in person, or with reasonable excuse to supply some other fit man to do it. A knight taken or sent on military service shall be excused from castle-guard for the period of this service.

(30) No sheriff, royal official, or other person shall take horses or carts for transport from any free man, without his consent.

(31) Neither we nor any royal official will take wood for our castle, or for any other purpose, without the consent of the owner.

(32) We will not keep the lands of people convicted of felony in our hand for longer than a year and a day, after which they shall be returned to the lords of the "fees" concerned.

(33) All fish-weirs shall be removed from the Thames, the Medway, and throughout the whole of England, except on the sea coast.

(34) The writ called *precipe* shall not in future be issued to anyone in respect of any holding of land, if a free man could thereby be deprived of the right of trial in his own lord's court.

(35) There shall be standard measures of wine, ale, and corn (the London quarter), throughout the kingdom. There shall also be a standard width of dyed cloth, russett, and haberject, namely two ells within the selvedges. Weights are to be standardised similarly.

(36) In future nothing shall be paid or accepted for the issue of a writ of inquisition of life or limbs. It shall be given gratis, and not refused.

(37) If a man holds land of the Crown by "fee-farm," "socage," or "burgage," and also holds land of someone else for knight's service, we will not have guardianship of his heir, nor of the land that belongs to the other person's "fee," by virtue of the "fee-farm," "socage," or "burgage," unless the "fee-farm" owes knight's service. We will not have the guardianship of a man's heir, or of land that he holds of someone else, by reason of any small property that he may hold of the Crown for a service of knives, arrows, or the like.

(38) In future no official shall place a man on trial upon his own unsupported statement, without producing credible witnesses to the truth of it.

(39) No free man shall be seized or imprisoned, or stripped of his rights or possessions, or outlawed or exiled, or deprived of his standing in any other way, nor will we proceed with force against him, or send others to do so, except by the lawful judgement of his equals or by the law of the land.

(40) To no one will we sell, to no one deny or delay right or justice.

(41) All merchants may enter or leave England unharmed and without fear, and may stay or travel within it, by land or water, for purposes of trade, free from all illegal exactions, in accordance with ancient and lawful customs. This, however, does not apply in time of war to merchants from a country that is at war with us. Any such merchants found in our country at the outbreak of war shall be detained without injury to their

persons or property, until we or our chief justice have discovered how our own merchants are being treated in the country at war with us. If our own merchants are safe they shall be safe too.

(42) In future it shall be lawful for any man to leave and return to our kingdom unharmed and without fear, by land or water, preserving his allegiance to us, except in time of war, for some short period, for the common benefit of the realm. People that have been imprisoned or outlawed in accordance with the law of the land, people from a country that is at war with us, and merchants—who shall be dealt with as stated above—are excepted from this provision.

(43) If a man holds lands of any "escheat" such as the "honour" of Wallingford, Nottingham, Boulogne, Lancaster, or of other "escheats" in our hand that are baronies, at his death his heir shall give us only the "relief" and service that he would have made to the baron, had the barony been in the baron's hand. We will hold the "escheat" in the same manner as the baron held it.

(44) People who live outside the forest need not in future appear before the royal justices of the forest in answer to general summonses, unless they are actually involved in proceedings or are sureties for someone who has been seized for a forest offence.

(45) We will appoint as justices, constables, sheriffs, or other officials, only men that know the law of the realm and are minded to keep it well.

(46) All barons who have founded abbeys, and have charters of English kings or ancient tenure as evidence of this, may have guardianship of them when there is no abbot, as is their due.

(47) All forests that have been created in our reign shall at once be disafforested. River-banks that have been enclosed in our reign shall be treated similarly.

(48) All evil customs relating to forests and warrens, foresters, warreners, sheriffs and their servants, or river-banks and their wardens, are at once to be investigated in every county by twelve sworn knights of the

county, and within forty days of their enquiry the evil customs are to be abolished completely and irrevocably. But we, or our chief justice if we are not in England, are first to be informed.

(49) We will at once return all hostages and charters delivered up to us by Englishmen as security for peace or for loyal service.

(50) We will remove completely from their offices the kinsmen of Gerard de Athée, and in future they shall hold no offices in England. The people in question are Engelard de Cigogné, Peter, Guy, and Andrew de Chanceaux, Guy de Cigogné, Geoffrey de Martigny and his brothers, Philip Marc and his brothers, with Geoffrey his nephew, and all their followers.

(51) As soon as peace is restored, we will remove from the kingdom all the foreign knights, bowmen, their attendants, and the mercenaries that have come to it, to its harm, with horses and arms.

(52) To any man whom we have deprived or dispossessed of lands, castles, liberties, or rights, without the lawful judgement of his equals, we will at once restore these. In cases of dispute the matter shall be resolved by the judgement of the twenty-five barons referred to below in the clause for securing the peace (§ 61). In cases, however, where a man was deprived or dispossessed of something without the lawful judgement of his equals by our father King Henry or our brother King Richard, and it remains in our hands or is held by others under our warranty, we shall have respite for the period commonly allowed to Crusaders, unless a lawsuit had been begun, or an enquiry had been made at our order, before we took the Cross as a Crusader. On our return from the Crusade, or if we abandon it, we will at once render justice in full.

(53) We shall have similar respite in rendering justice in connexion with forests that are to be disafforested, or to remain forests, when these were first afforested by our father Henry or our brother Richard; with the guardianship of lands in another person's "fee," when we have hitherto had this by virtue of a "fee" held of us for knight's service by a third party; and with abbeys founded in another person's "fee," in which the lord of the "fee" claims to own a right. On our return from the Crusade, or if

we abandon it, we will at once do full justice to complaints about these matters.

(54) No one shall be arrested or imprisoned on the appeal of a woman for the death of any person except her husband.

(55) All fines that have been given to us unjustly and against the law of the land, and all fines that we have exacted unjustly, shall be entirely remitted or the matter decided by a majority judgement of the twenty-five barons referred to below in the clause for securing the peace (§ 61) together with Stephen, archbishop of Canterbury, if he can be present, and such others as he wishes to bring with him. If the archbishop cannot be present, proceedings shall continue without him, provided that if any of the twenty-five barons has been involved in a similar suit himself, his judgement shall be set aside, and someone else chosen and sworn in his place, as a substitute for the single occasion, by the rest of the twenty-five.

(56) If we have deprived or dispossessed any Welshmen of lands, liberties, or anything else in England or in Wales, without the lawful judgement of their equals, these are at once to be returned to them. A dispute on this point shall be determined in the Marches by the judgement of equals. English law shall apply to holdings of land in England, Welsh law to those in Wales, and the law of the Marches to those in the Marches. The Welsh shall treat us and ours in the same way.

(57) In cases where a Welshman was deprived or dispossessed of anything, without the lawful judgement of his equals, by our father King Henry or our brother King Richard, and it remains in our hands or is held by others under our warranty, we shall have respite for the period commonly allowed to Crusaders, unless a lawsuit had been begun, or an enquiry had been made at our order, before we took the Cross as a Crusader. But on our return from the Crusade, or if we abandon it, we will at once do full justice according to the laws of Wales and the said regions.

(58) We will at once return the son of Llywelyn, all Welsh hostages, and the charters delivered to us as security for the peace.

(59) With regard to the return of the sisters and hostages of Alexander, king of Scotland, his liberties and his rights, we will treat him in the same way as our other barons of England, unless it appears from the charters that we hold from his father William, formerly king of Scotland, that he should be treated otherwise. This matter shall be resolved by the judgement of his equals in our court.

(60) All these customs and liberties that we have granted shall be observed in our kingdom in so far as concerns our own relations with our subjects. Let all men of our kingdom, whether clergy or laymen, observe them similarly in their relations with their own men.

(61) SINCE WE HAVE GRANTED ALL THESE THINGS for God, for the better ordering of our kingdom, and to allay the discord that has arisen between us and our barons, and since we desire that they shall be enjoyed in their entirety, with lasting strength, for ever, we give and grant to the barons the following security:

The barons shall elect twenty-five of their number to keep, and cause to be observed with all their might, the peace and liberties granted and confirmed to them by this charter.

If we, our chief justice, our officials, or any of our servants offend in any respect against any man, or transgress any of the articles of the peace or of this security, and the offence is made known to four of the said twenty-five barons, they shall come to us—or in our absence from the kingdom to the chief justice—to declare it and claim immediate redress. If we, or in our absence abroad the chief justice, make no redress within forty days, reckoning from the day on which the offence was declared to us or to him, the four barons shall refer the matter to the rest of the twenty-five barons, who may distrain upon and assail us in every way possible, with the support of the whole community of the land, by seizing our castles, lands, possessions, or anything else saving only our own person and those of the queen and our children, until they have secured such redress as they have determined upon. Having secured the redress, they may then resume their normal obedience to us.

Any man who so desires may take an oath to obey the commands of the twenty-five barons for the achievement of these ends, and to join with them in assailing us to the utmost of his power. We give public and free permission to take this oath to any man who so desires, and at no time will we prohibit any man from taking it. Indeed, we will compel any of our subjects who are unwilling to take it to swear it at our command.

If one of the twenty-five barons dies or leaves the country, or is prevented in any other way from discharging his duties, the rest of them shall choose another baron in his place, at their discretion, who shall be duly sworn in as they were.

In the event of disagreement among the twenty-five barons on any matter referred to them for decision, the verdict of the majority present shall have the same validity as a unanimous verdict of the whole twenty-five, whether these were all present or some of those summoned were unwilling or unable to appear.

The twenty-five barons shall swear to obey all the above articles faithfully, and shall cause them to be obeyed by others to the best of their power.

We will not seek to procure from anyone, either by our own efforts or those of a third party, anything by which any part of these concessions or liberties might be revoked or diminished. Should such a thing be procured, it shall be null and void and we will at no time make use of it, either ourselves or through a third party.

(62) We have remitted and pardoned fully to all men any ill-will, hurt, or grudges that have arisen between us and our subjects, whether clergy or laymen, since the beginning of the dispute. We have in addition remitted fully, and for our own part have also pardoned, to all clergy and laymen any offences committed as a result of the said dispute between Easter in the sixteenth year of our reign (i.e. 1215) and the restoration of peace.

In addition we have caused letters patent to be made for the barons, bearing witness to this security and to the concessions set out above, over the seals of Stephen archbishop of Canterbury, Henry archbishop of Dublin, the other bishops named above, and Master Pandulf.

(63) IT IS ACCORDINGLY OUR WISH AND COMMAND that the English Church shall be free, and that men in our kingdom shall have and keep all these liberties, rights, and concessions, well and peaceably in their fulness and entirety for them and their heirs, of us and our heirs, in all things and all places for ever.

Both we and the barons have sworn that all this shall be observed in good faith and without deceit. Witness the abovementioned people and many others.

Given by our hand in the meadow that is called Runnymede, between Windsor and Staines, on the fifteenth day of June in the seventeenth year of our reign (i.e. 1215: the new regnal year began on 28 May).

Source and Further Information

G. R. C. Davis, *Magna Carta*, Revised Edition, British Library, 1989.

Notes

Chapter 1: Introduction

1. *Boumediene v. Bush*, 128 S.Ct. 2229, 2244 (2008).

2. Kenton Worcester, "Editor's Introduction to Magna Carta Symposium," *PS: Political Science and Politics* 43 (2010): 451.

3. J. C. Holt, *Magna Carta* (New York: Cambridge University Press, 1965), 156.

4. Creation of "forests" by the Crown placed certain lands beyond the public's use and made it illegal for the public to access those lands (to do so was a violation of "forest law"). Thus, forestation and disafforestation became controversial, and the barons obtained concessions regarding the forestation process.

5. Holt, *Magna Carta*, 16.

6. Ibid., 102.

7. Ibid., 150.

8. Ibid., 180.

9. Coronation Charter of Henry I, 1100, www.fordham.edu/halsall/source/hcoronation.asp (accessed December 30, 2013).

10. Holt, *Magna Carta*, 206.

11. Ibid., 230.

12. Some opinions use the spelling "Magna Charta."

13. 13 U.S. 388, slip op. at 30 (1815).

14. 59 U.S. 396, 402 (1856).

15. 357 U.S. 116 (1958).

16. 356 U.S. 86, 100 (1958).

17. 386 U.S. 213, 223–224 (1966).

18. 410 U.S. 19, 29 (1973) (Douglas, J., dissenting).

19. 463 U.S. 277, 284 (1983).

20. 492 U.S. 257, 268 (1989).

21. 581 U.S. 261, 284 (1997).

22. 131 S.Ct. 2488, 2499 (2011).

23. 132 S.Ct. 694, 702 (2012).

24. Akhil Reed Amar, *America's Unwritten Constitution: The Precedents and Principles We Live By* (New York: Basic Books, 2012), 12–13.

25. Ibid., 247.

26. Ibid., 481.

27. Louis Hartz, *The Liberal Tradition in America* (New York: Harcourt Brace Jovanovich, 1955).

28. Adrian Vermeule, "Common Law Constitutionalism and the Limits of Reason," *Columbia Law Review* 107 (2007): 1482.

29. Amar, *America's Unwritten Constitution*, 13.

30. Frank Michelman, "Brennan and Democracy," *California Law Review* 86 (1998): 399.

31. Ibid., 427.

32. Antonin Scalia, "A Dialogue on Statutory and Constitutional Interpretation," *George Washington Law Review* 80 (2012): 1613, 1616.

33. Vermeule, "Common Law Constitutionalism and the Limits of Reason," 1482.

34. Ibid., 1518.

35. Frederick Gedicks, "An Originalist Defense of Substantive Due Process: Magna Carta, Higher Law Constitutionalism, and the Fifth Amendment," *Emory Law Journal* 58 (2009): 606.

36. Ibid., 613.

37. Ibid.

38. Kate Zernike, "Christie Wants Voters to Decide on Gay Marriage," *New York Times*, 24 January 2012, www.nytimes.com/2012/01/25/nyregion/christie-wants-new-jersey-voters-to-decide-on-gay-marriage.html (accessed January 3, 2014).

39. David Dyzenhaus, *The Constitution of Law: Legality in a Time of Emergency* (New York: Cambridge University Press, 2006).

40. *Boumediene v. Bush*, supra, at 2259.

41. Dyzenhaus, *The Constitution of Law*, 39.

42. Bruce Ackerman, "The Emergency Constitution," *Yale Law Journal* 113 (2004): 1029.

43. Dyzenhaus, *The Constitution of Law*, 42.

44. Edward Jenks, "The Myth of Magna Carta," *Independent Review* 4 (1904): 260.

45. Ibid., 269.

46. Ibid., 272.

47. James Wert, "With a Little Help from a Friend: Habeas Corpus and the Magna Carta after Runnymede," *PS: Political Science and Politics* 43 (2010): 475.

48. Jenks, "The Myth of Magna Carta," 271.

49. Akhil Reed Amar, *America's Constitution: A Biography* (New York: Random House, 2005), 18.

50. Edward Purcell, *Brandeis and the Progressive Constitution* (New Haven, CT: Yale University Press, 2000), 181.

Chapter 2: Early Theoretical Foundations

1. I have borrowed the phrase "common law mind" from James Stoner's influential work *Common Law and Liberal Theory* (Lawrence: University Press of Kansas, 1992), 163.

2. Ibid., 7.

3. Ibid.

4. Ibid.

5. Duncan Kennedy, "The Structure of Blackstone's Commentaries," *Buffalo Law Review* 28 (1979): 261.

6. Stoner, *Common Law and Liberal Theory*, 23.

7. I have mentioned this rule of construction in reference to impeachment proceedings in the U.S. Congress, as cited by Akhil Reed Amar, *America's Unwritten Constitution: The Precedents and Principles We Live By* (New York: Basic Books, 2012), 7. We will see it again in *City of London v. Wood*, 12 Mod. 669, 88 Eng. Rep. 1592 (1702). The "judge in its own cause" maxim has a lineage of its own in the common law, providing the specific rationale for voiding acts of government through judicial review. Also, King James I of England cited it in "The Trew Law of Free Monarchies," in *Introduction to Contemporary Civilization in the West*, ed. Justus Buchler et al. (New York: Columbia University Press, 1960), 937. For a contemporary application, see Robert Pallitto and William Weaver, *Presidential Secrecy and the Law* (Baltimore: Johns Hopkins University Press, 2007), 198.

8. Frederick Gedicks, "An Originalist Defense of Substantive Due Process: Magna Carta, Higher Law Constitutionalism, and the Fifth Amendment," *Emory Law Journal* 58 (2009): 604.

9. A case decided nearly 400 years later provides an interesting comparison to *Bonham's Case*. In *Bob Jones University v. U.S.*, 461 U.S. 574 (1983), Bob Jones University, a private religious institution, challenged an action by the Internal Revenue Service revoking its tax-exempt status. The IRS adopted the common law definition of "charitable purpose" and decided that an institution acting against public policy (such as the racially segregated university here) did not serve a charitable purpose. Bob Jones argued that Congress had not given the IRS the authority to define "charitable purpose" in this way, but the Supreme Court disagreed and ruled in favor of the IRS. So this case involved an agency applying positive law, as did *Bonham's Case*. Similar to *Bonham's Case*, the *Bob Jones* decision upheld use of the common law to construe positive law. The difference, of course, is that the government, not the individual litigant, was the party seeking to apply the common law in *Bob Jones*. And the Supreme Court ruled *against* the individual and in favor of the government—the opposite of the result for *Bonham*. Though the parties and their interests lined up in a rather unusual way in the *Bob Jones* case, the end result was that common law doctrine allowed for the resolution of a public dispute with larger social ramifications.

10. 5 U.S. 137 (1803).

11. Edward Corwin, "The 'Higher Law' Background of American Constitutional Law," *Harvard Law Review* 62 (1928): 149.

12. Gary McDowell, "Coke, Corwin and the Constitution: The 'Higher Law Background' Reconsidered," *Review of Politics* 55 (1993): 399.

13. Ibid., 402.

14. See, for example, ibid., 405.

15. Rogers Smith, *Liberalism and American Constitutional Law* (Cambridge, MA: Harvard University Press, 1985), 22.

16. John Phillip Reid lists the alternative theories for "why nature was a constitutional authority establishing the right to rights." Reid, "The Authority of Rights at the American Founding," in *The Nature of Rights at the American Founding and Beyond*, ed. Barry Alan Shain (Charlottesville: University Press of Virginia, 2007), 94. Natural law is founded in God, in reason, in human essence, and in the state of nature. Reid's list closely tracks the theoretical grounds I have listed in this section.

17. Mary Sarah Bilder, "Colonial Constitutionalism and Constitutional Law," in *Transformations in American Legal History: Essays in Honor of Professor Morton J. Horwitz*, ed. Daniel W. Hamilton and Alfred L. Brophy (Cambridge, MA: Harvard University Press, 2009), 29. Bilder considers this claim to be a myth.

18. Ibid., 35.

19. Ibid.

20. A. E. Dick Howard, *The Road from Runnymede* (Charlottesville: University of Virginia Press, 1968), 30.

21. Ibid., 37–39.

22. Ibid., 76.

23. Ibid., 79.

24. James Hutson, "The Emergence of the Modern Concept of a Right in America," in *The Nature of Rights at the American Founding and Beyond*, ed. Barry Alan Shain (Charlottesville: University Press of Virginia, 2007), 42.

25. Reid, "The Authority of Rights at the American Founding," 90.

26. Ibid., 92.

27. Richard Primus, "Introduction to the Nature of American Rights," in *The Nature of Rights at the American Founding and Beyond*, ed. Barry Alan Shain (Charlottesville: University Press of Virginia, 2007), 17.

28. Reid, "The Authority of Rights at the American Founding," 82.

29. Ibid., 100.

30. Primus, "Introduction to the Nature of American Rights," 19.

31. Hutson, "The Emergence of the Modern Concept of a Right in America," 52.

32. Stoner, *Common Law and Liberal Theory*, 188.

33. Bilder, "Colonial Constitutionalism and Constitutional Law," 44.

34. Howard, *The Road from Runnymede*, 12.

35. Blackstone, like Coke, served in Parliament and as a judge; he also lectured on law at Oxford.

36. Sir William Blackstone, *Commentaries on the Law of England*, 4 vols. (London, 1809), 1:91.

37. Kennedy, "The Structure of Blackstone's Commentaries," 210.

38. Antonio Gramsci, *Selections from the Prison Notebooks* (New York: International Publishers, 1971).

39. Kennedy, "The Structure of Blackstone's Commentaries," 219.

40. Ibid., 259–260.

41. Morton Horwitz, *The Transformation of American Law, 1780–1860* (Cambridge, MA: Harvard University Press, 1977), 3–4.

42. Ibid., xii.

43. See Duncan Kennedy, "Freedom and Constraint in Adjudication: A Critical Phenomenology of Judging," *Journal of Legal Education* 36 (1986): 518.

44. McDowell, "Coke, Corwin and the Constitution," 416.

45. David Thomas Konig, "Constitutional Contexts: The Theory of History and the Process of Constitutional Change in Revolutionary America," in *Constitutionalism and American Culture: Writing the New Constitutional History*, ed. Sandra F. VanBurkleo, Kermit L. Hall, and Robert J. Kaczorowski (Lawrence: University Press of Kansas, 2002), 21.

46. Smith, *Liberalism and American Constitutional Law*, 31.

Chapter 3: The Slavery Question

1. See, for example, the Kentucky case of *Rankin v. Lydia* (2 A.K. Marshall's Rep.), cited in *Dred Scott v. Sandford,* 60 U.S. 393, 536 (McLean, J., dissenting).

2. 13 N.C. 263 (1829), excerpted in Robert Pallitto, *Torture and State Violence in the United States: A Short Documentary History* (Baltimore: Johns Hopkins University Press, 2011), 58.

3. The word "excessively" is key here, for in pre–Civil War statutes "moderate correction" of slaves was lawful, and the criminal nature of a beating lay only in the degree of force used rather than in the act of beating a slave. Even if a slave died under "moderate correction," the action was lawful if moderate. Ibid., 61. See also Colin Dayan, *The Story of Cruel and Unusual* (Cambridge, MA: Boston Review Press, 2007).

4. Pallitto, *Torture and State Violence in the United States.*

5. Ibid.

6. Ibid., 60.

7. William Wiecek, *The Sources of Antislavery Constitutionalism* (Ithaca, NY: Cornell University Press, 1977), 282.

8. Stuart Streichler, *Justice Curtis in the Civil War Era: At the Crossroads of American Constitutionalism* (Charlottesville: University Press of Virginia, 2005), 100.

9. Ibid, 118.

10. Ibid., 39.

11. *Dred Scott v. Sandford*, Curtis, J., dissenting

12. Streichler, *Justice Curtis in the Civil War Era*, 146.

13. Ibid, xx.

14. Ibid., 205.

15. Ibid., 206.

16. *Sommersett v. Stewart*, 20 How. 79 (1772).

17. A. Leon Higginbotham, *In the Matter of Color: Race and the American Legal Process* (New York: Oxford University Press, 1978), 333.

18. Ibid., 334.

19. Ibid., 340.

20. *Sommersett*, supra. In a striking coincidence, the "inconvenience" cited here by Mansfield resulting to whites as a consequence of recognizing the rights of blacks was cited again, in 1974, by Justice Thurgood Marshall as Marshall considered the busing issue. "The inconvenience of some," Marshall wrote in his dissent in *Milliken v. Bradley*, "cannot be allowed to stand in the way of the rights of others." One wonders whether this choice of words on Marshall's part, almost exactly 200 years later, was a deliberate reference to *Sommersett*. This statement was cited in Peter Irons, *Jim Crow's Children* (New York: Penguin Books, 2003), 245.

21. Higginbotham, *In the Matter of Color*, 355.

22. Wiecek, *The Sources of Antislavery Constitutionalism*, 35.

23. *Rex v. Allen*, 116 Eng. Rep. 179 (1827). Wiecek calls this the "reattachment" doctrine, whereby a slave returning from free soil to a slave state reacquires slave status. Wiecek, *The Sources of Antislavery Constitutionalism*, 36–37.

24. Higginbotham, *In the Matter of Color*, 362.

25. Ibid. 367.

26. 23 U.S. 66 (1825).

27. Wiecek, *The Sources of Antislavery Constitutionalism*, 286.

28. 60 U.S. 393, 550–557 (McLean, J., dissenting).

29. 35 Mass. 193 (1836).

30. 41 U.S. 539, 610 (1842).

31. Ibid., 611.

32. Ibid., 612.

33. Ibid., 616.

34. See, for example, *Prigg*, 623.

35. Ibid., 624.

36. Wiecek, *The Sources of Antislavery Constitutionalism*, 159.

37. Justin Buckley Dyer, "Slavery and the Magna Carta in the

Development of Anglo-American Constitutionalism," *PS: Political Science and Politics* 43 (2010): 481.

38. Ibid.

39. Ibid.

40. Higginbotham, *In the Matter of Color*, 334.

41. *Elkison v. Deliesseline*, 8 Fed. Cas. 493 (No. 4366) C.C.D.S.S.C. (1827), cited in Wiecek, *The Sources of Antislavery Constitutionalism*, 134.

42. 60 U.S. 393, 404 (1857).

43. Ibid., 407.

44. See, for example, 412, 426, 437, 446.

45. For example, Mark Graber, *Dred Scott and the Problem of Constitutional Evil* (New York: Cambridge University Press, 2006).

46. Streichler, *Justice Curtis in the Civil War Era*, 142.

47. *Dred Scott*, 60 U.S. at 626–627.

48. Ibid., 627.

49. Ibid., 404.

50. Streichler, *Justice Curtis in the Civil War Era*, 127.

51. Ibid., 150.

52. Wiecek, *The Sources of Antislavery Constitutionalism*, 6.

53. Ibid., 252.

54. Ibid., 259.

55. Ibid., 274.

Chapter 4: Federal Common Law, Legal Realism, and the Magna Carta Tradition

1. Noah Feldman, *Scorpions: The Battles and Triumphs of FDR's Great Supreme Court Justices* (New York: Twelve, 2010), 406.

2. Edward Purcell, *Brandeis and the Progressive Constitution* (New Haven, CT: Yale University Press, 2000), 13.

3. 198 U.S. 45.

4. 10 U.S. 87 (1810).

5. 17 U.S. 122 (1819).

6. 41 U.S. 1 (1842).

7. Henry Hart and Herbert Wechsler, *The Federal Courts and the Federal System*, 2nd ed. (Mineola, NY: Foundation Press, 1973), 770.

8. In order for the federal courts to have subject-matter jurisdiction over a case, it must present a question of federal law (federal question

jurisdiction) or arise from a dispute between citizens of two different states (diversity jurisdiction)

9. *Swift v. Tyson*, 42 U.S. at 18.

10. Purcell, *Brandeis and the Progressive Constitution*, 47.

11. Ibid.

12. 149 U.S. 368 (1893).

13. 206 U.S. 46 (1907).

14. 158 U.S. 564 (1895).

15. 276 U.S. 518 (1928).

16. Charles Alan Wright, *The Law of Federal Courts*, 4th ed. (St. Paul, MN: West, 1983), 351.

17. *Black and White Taxicab*, 528.

18. Ibid., 535.

19. Ibid., 533.

20. Hart and Wechsler, *The Federal Courts and the Federal System*, 800.

21. *Erie v. Tompkins*, 304 U.S. 64, 75 (1938).

22. Purcell, *Brandeis and the Progressive Constitution*, 97–99.

23. *Erie v. Tompkins*, 304 U.S. 64, 78 (1938).

24. Ibid., 79.

25. John Chipman Gray, "The Nature and Sources of the Law," in *American Legal Realism*, ed. William W. Fisher III, Morton J. Horwitz, and Thomas A. Reed (New York: Oxford University Press, 1993), 37.

26. Ibid., 36.

27. *Muller v. Oregon*, 208 U.S. 412 (1908).

28. The result for the parties in *Erie* was a different story. The case was remanded to be decided under the new rule that favored the railroad (and disadvantaged the individual) in this case. Thus the long-term and short-term results of the case were quite different.

29. Purcell, *Brandeis and the Progressive Constitution*, 142.

30. Ibid., 105.

31. Quoted in Hart and Wechsler, *The Federal Courts and the Federal System*, 707.

32. *Lochner v. New York*, 198 U.S. 45, 75 (1905) (Holmes, J., dissenting).

33. Oliver Wendell Holmes, "The Path of the Law," in *American Legal Realism*, ed. William W. Fisher III, Morton J. Horwitz, and Thomas A. Reed (New York: Oxford University Press, 1993), 22.

34. William W. Fisher III, Morton J. Horwitz, and Thomas A. Reed, "Introduction," *American Legal Realism*, ed. William W. Fisher III,

Morton J. Horwitz, and Thomas A. Reed (New York: Oxford University Press, 1993), xiii.

35. Oliver Wendell Holmes, *The Common Law* (Boston: Little, Brown, 1881), 1.

36. Holmes, "The Path of the Law," 21.

37. Ibid.

38. Roscoe Pound, "Liberty of Contract," in *American Legal Realism*, ed. William W. Fisher III, Morton J. Horwitz, and Thomas A. Reed (New York: Oxford University Press, 1993), 33.

39. Ibid., 31–32.

40. Roscoe Pound, "Law in Books and Law in Action," in *American Legal Realism*, ed. William W. Fisher III, Morton J. Horwitz, and Thomas A. Reed (New York: Oxford University Press, 1993), 43.

41. Roscoe Pound, "The Call for a Realist Jurisprudence," in *American Legal Realism*, ed. William W. Fisher III, Morton J. Horwitz, and Thomas A. Reed (New York: Oxford University Press, 1993), 61.

42. Karl Llewellyn, "A Realistic Jurisprudence—The Next Step," in *American Legal Realism*, ed. William W. Fisher III, Morton J. Horwitz, and Thomas A. Reed (New York: Oxford University Press, 1993), 54.

43. Karl Llewellyn, "Some Realism about Realism—Responding to Dean Pound," in *American Legal Realism*, ed. William W. Fisher III, Morton J. Horwitz, and Thomas A. Reed (New York: Oxford University Press, 1993), 73.

44. Jerome Frank, "Law and the Modern Mind," in *American Legal Realism*, ed. William W. Fisher III, Morton J. Horwitz, and Thomas A. Reed (New York: Oxford University Press, 1993), 210.

45. Herman Oliphant, "Return to Stare Decisis," in *American Legal Realism*, ed. William W. Fisher III, Morton J. Horwitz, and Thomas A. Reed (New York: Oxford University Press, 1993), 199.

46. Nancy Fraser, "Foucault on Modern Power: Empirical Insights and Normative Confusions," *Praxis International* 3 (1981): 272.

47. Pound's "Liberty of Contract," for example, addressed constitutional method.

48. Llewellyn, "Some Realism about Realism," 75.

49. Llewellyn, "A Realistic Jurisprudence," 53.

50. Feldman, *Scorpions*, 364.

51. Louise Weinberg, "Federal Common Law," *Northwestern University Law Review* 83 (1989): 807.

52. Ibid., 819.

53. Ibid., 807.

54. Ibid., 808.

55. Ibid., 848.

56. *Southern Pacific Co. v. Jensen*, 244 U.S. 205, 222 (1917) (Holmes, J. dissenting).

57. Weinberg, "Federal Common Law," 834.

Chapter 5: The Warren Court, Civil Rights, and the Incorporation Controversy

1. Louise Weinberg, "Federal Common Law," *Northwestern University Law Review* 83 (1989): 834.

2. William Brennan, "Why Have a Bill of Rights?," *Valparaiso Law Review* 26 (1991): 1.

3. Noah Feldman, *Scorpions: The Battles and Triumphs of FDR's Great Supreme Court Justices* (New York: Twelve, 2010), 373.

4. The factual backgrounds of these cases preceding *Brown* are detailed in Peter Irons's excellent book *Jim Crow's Children* (New York: Penguin Books, 2003).

5. 339 U.S. 629 (1950).

6. *McLaurin v. Oklahoma State Regents*, 339 U.S. 637 (1950).

7. 163 U.S. 537 (1896).

8. *Roberts v. Boston*, 59 Mass. 198 (1850).

9. 347 U.S. 483 (1954), 492–293.

10. Edward Purcell, *Brandeis and the Progressive Constitution* (New Haven, CT: Yale University Press, 2000), 259.

11. Rogers Smith, *Civic Ideals: Conflicting Visions of Citizenship in U.S. History* (New Haven, CT: Yale University Press, 1997), 26.

12. Michael Belknap, "The Warren Court and Equality," in *Constitutionalism and American Culture: Writing the New Constitutional History*, ed. Sandra F. VanBurkleo, Kermit L. Hall, and Robert J. Kaczorowski (Lawrence: University Press of Kansas, 2002), 213.

13. 367 U.S. 643 (1961).

14. 384 U.S. 436 (1966).

15. 372 U.S. 335 (1963).

16. Hugo Black, dissenting in *Adamson v. California*, quoted in Tony Freyer, "Hugo L. Black and the Warren Court in Retrospect," in *The Warren Court in Historical and Political Perspective*, ed. Mark Tushnet (Charlottesville: University Press of Virginia, 1993), 101.

17. *Wolf v. Colorado*, 338 U.S. 25 (1949), 27. This was Frankfurter's view in 1949. Earlier, he had spoken quite differently about the Due Process Clause and, as Bickel notes, even suggested at one point that it ought to be repealed. Alexander Bickel, *The Supreme Court and the Idea of Progress* (New Haven, CT: Yale University Press, 1978), 26.

18. *Griswold v. Connecticut*, 381 U.S. 479 (1965), 481.

19. Ibid., 484.

20. Ibid., 485.

21. 410 U.S. 113 (1973).

22. 539 U.S. 558 (2003).

23. Melvin Urofsky, "William O. Douglas as Common Law Judge," in *The Warren Court in Historical and Political Perspective*, ed. Mark Tushnet (Charlottesville: University Press of Virginia, 1993), 74.

24. Ibid.

25. Ibid., 69.

26. Ibid., 74.

27. Ibid., 78.

28. Ibid., 85.

29. 372 U.S. 391 (1963).

30. 372 U.S. at 438.

31. 372 U.S. at 423.

32. 372. U.S. at 402.

33. 372 U.S. at 423.

34. 372 U.S. at 426.

35. 372 U.S. at 441.

36. 369 U.S. 186 (1961).

37. 383 U.S. 663 (1966).

38. Ibid., 369.

39. 384 U.S. 641 (1966).

40. Purcell, *Brandeis and the Progressive Constitution*, 259.

41. Irons describes a number of instances where opposition stemmed from within the federal judiciary as well. At times, federal judges balked at enforcing the Court's orders, supporting instead recalcitrant state officials' pleas for delay. See, for example, Irons, *Jim Crow's Children*, 206.

42. Bickel, *The Supreme Court and the Idea of Progress*, 13.

43. Ibid., 47.

44. Ibid., 87.

45. Ibid., 19.

46. Ibid.
47. Ibid., 87.
48. Ibid., 81.
49. Ibid., 82.
50. Brennan, "Why Have a Bill of Rights?," 11–12.
51. Bickel, *The Supreme Court and the Idea of Progress*, 37.
52. Urofsky, "William O. Douglas as Common Law Judge," 78.
53. Akhil Reed Amar, *America's Unwritten Constitution* (New York: Basic Books, 2012), 146–149.
54. Purcell, *Brandeis and the Progressive Constitution*, 230–233.
55. Ibid., 235.
56. Ibid., 236.
57. Ibid., 250–251.
58. Ibid., 257.
59. Bickel, *The Supreme Court and the Idea of Progress*, 137.
60. Ibid., 98.
61. Amar, *America's Unwritten Constitution*, 198.
62. Bickel, *The Supreme Court and the Idea of Progress*, 90–91.

Chapter 6: The Rehnquist Court and Habeas Corpus Retrenchment

1. David Shapiro, "Mr. Justice Rehnquist: A Preliminary View," *Harvard Law Review* 90 (1976): 233. Shapiro gave his evaluation of Rehnquist's jurisprudence before Rehnquist was elevated to chief justice, but it remained accurate and is cited widely.
2. Marshall Hartman and Jeanette Nyden use the term "retrenchment" specifically in reference to the habeas rulings of the Rehnquist Court. Hartman and Nyden, "Habeas Corpus and the New Federalism after the Antiterrorism and Effective Death Penalty Act of 1996," *John Marshall Law Review* 30 (1997): 343.
3. Jack Balkin and Sanford Levinson, "Understanding the Constitutional Revolution," *Virginia Law Review* 87 (2001): 1045.
4. Steven Smith, "The Rehnquist Court and Criminal Procedure," *University of Colorado Law Review* 73 (2002): 1337.
5. Mark Tushnet, "The King of France with Forty Thousand Men: *Felker v. Turpin* and the Supreme Court's Deliberative Processes," *University of Chicago Supreme Court Review* 1996 (1996): 170.
6. *Teague v. Lane*, 489 U.S. 288 (1989).

7. Stephen Feldman, "Diagnosing Power: Postmodernism in Legal Scholarship and Judicial Practice (with an Emphasis on the *Teague* Rule against New Rules in Habeas Corpus Cases)," *Northwestern University Law Review* 88 (1994): 1049.

8. A peremptory challenge allows an attorney to dismiss a potential juror without giving a reason.

9. *Teague*, 489 U.S. at 301.

10. Ibid.

11. Ibid., 333.

12. Feldman, "Diagnosing Power," 1067.

13. Ibid., 1066–1069.

14. Ibid., 1079.

15. 501 U.S. 722 (1991).

16. 504 U.S. 1 (1992).

17. 507 U.S. 619 (1993).

18. 506 U.S. 390 (1993).

19. 372 U.S. 293, 317 (1963).

20. *Herrera*, 506 U.S. 390, 404.

21. Ibid., 417.

22. Ibid., 398.

23. Ibid., 31.

24. 342 U.S. 165, 172 (1952).

25. Henry Friendly, "Is Innocence Irrelevant? Collateral Attack on Criminal Judgments," *University of Chicago Law Review* 38 (1970): 142.

26. *Herrera*, 506 U.S. 390, 446.

27. The Antiterrorism and Effective Death Penalty Act of 1996, Public Law No. 104-132, 110 Stat. 1214.

28. The "preclusion of review" provision was tested in a case heard shortly after the AEDPA was signed into law. In *Felker v. Turpin*, 518 U.S. 1051 (1996), the Court ruled that the AEDPA's preclusion of Supreme Court habeas review on petition for certiorari was constitutional, and that the Court could still take original jurisdiction of a petition filed in the Supreme Court itself. Ultimately, Felker's petition itself was denied, and he was executed late in 1996.

29. Anthony Gregory, *The Power of Habeas Corpus in America: From the King's Prerogative to the War on Terror* (New York: Cambridge University Press for the Independent Institute, 2013), 179.

30. Information about the Innocence Project can be found at www.innocenceproject.org (accessed December 19, 2013).

31. 42 U.S.C. Section 1983 is a federal statute that provides the basis for a lawsuit when a person has suffered the deprivation of a federal statutory or constitutional right.

32. *District Attorney's Office v. Osborne*, 557 U.S. 52 (2009).

33. Ibid.

34. Smith, "The Rehnquist Court and Criminal Procedure," 1344–1345.

35. Ibid., 1360.

36. Ibid.

37. Gregory, *The Power of Habeas Corpus in America*, 35–37.

38. Ibid., 89.

Chapter 7: The War on Terror

1. The UCMJ, formerly the Articles of War, is a statute passed by Congress and modified numerous times by subsequent legislation.

2. 542 U.S. 507, 535 (2004).

3. Mark Denbeaux and Joshua Denbeaux, *No-Hearing Hearings* (2006), http://law.shu.edu/publications/guantanamoReports/final_no_hearing_hearings_report.pdf.

4. Ibid., 2.

5. Ibid., 3.

6. Ibid.

7. 542 U.S. 466 (2004).

8. 542 U.S. at 472.

9. 11 Stat. 2680.

10. 548 U.S. 557 (2006).

11. 120 Stat. 2600.

12. *Boumediene v. Bush*, 128 S.Ct. 2229, 2244 (2008).

13. Baher Azmy, "Executive Detention, *Boumediene* and the New Common Law of Habeas," *Iowa Law Review* 95 (2010): 447.

14. Benjamin Wittes, Robert Chesney, and Larkin Reynolds, *The Emerging Law of Detention 2.0: The Guantanamo Habeas Cases as Lawmaking*, 2012, www.brookings.edu/~/media/research/files/reports/2011/5/guantanamo%20wittes/chesney%20full%20text%20update32913.pdf (accessed December 5, 2013).

15. *Ali Ahmed v. Obama*, 613 F. Supp. 2d 51, 55 (D.D.C. 2009).

16. Ibid., 56.

17. 613 F. 3d 1102 (D.C. Cir. 2010).

18. Ibid., 1106.

19. Wittes, Chesney, and Reynolds, *The Emerging Law of Detention 2.0*, 121.

20. Ibid., 121.

21. Ibid., 95.

22. Ibid., 7. The case is *Parhat v. Gates*, 532 F. 3d 834 (D.C. Cir. 2008).

23. Ibid.

24. *Alwi v. Obama*, 132 S.Ct. 2739 (June 11, 2012); *Al Madhwani v. Obama*, 132 S.Ct. 2739 (June 11, 2012); *Almerfedi v. Obama*, 132 S.Ct. 2739 (June 11, 2012); *Uthman v. Obama*, 132 S.Ct. 2739 (June 11, 2012); *Al Bihani v. Obama*, 132 S.Ct. 2739 (June 11, 2012); *Al Kandari v. United States*, 132 S.Ct. 2741 (June 11, 2012); *Latif v. Obama*, 132 S.Ct. 2741 (June 11, 2012).

25. Transcript of panel discussion: "Boumediene's Legacy and the Fate of Guantanamo Detainees, July 17, 2012," www.constitutionproject.org/pdf/Transcript%20from%20Panel%20Discussion_Boumediene.pdf.

26. Karen DeYoung, "Afghan War's Approaching End Throws Legal Status of Detainees into Doubt," *Washington Post*, October 13, 2013, www.washingtonpost.com/world/national-security/afghan-wars-approaching-end-throws-legal-status-of-guantanamo-detainees-into-doubt/2013/10/18/758be516–2d0a-11e3–97a3-ff2758228523_story_1.html (accessed November 27, 2013).

27. Jane Mayer, *The Dark Side: How the War on Terror Turned into a War on American Ideals* (New York: Doubleday, 2008).

28. See, for example, Karen Greenberg and Josh Dratel, *The Torture Papers: The Road to Abu Ghraib* (New York: Cambridge University Press, 2005); Alfred McCoy, *Torture and Impunity* (Madison: University of Wisconsin Press, 2012); Robert Pallitto, *Torture and State Violence in the United States: A Short Documentary History* (Baltimore: Johns Hopkins University Press, 2011).

29. The Eighth Amendment prohibits cruel and unusual punishment; the Fifth and Fourteenth, as we have seen, guarantee due process of law. The Fifth Amendment also confers a privilege against self-incrimination. For the text of this reservation, see Pallitto, *Torture and State Violence in the United States*, 173.

30. 18 U.S.C. Section 2340.

31. Memorandum of Jay Bybee to Alberto Gonzales, August 1, 2002, http://f11.findlaw.com/news.findlaw.com/nytimes/docs/doj/bybee80102mem.pdf (accessed December 2, 2013).

32. Executive Order 13491, "Ensuring Lawful Interrogations," January 22, 2009, www.whitehouse.gov/the-press-office/ensuring-lawful-interrogations (accessed December 2, 2013).

33. Craig Whitlock, "Rendition Continues under Obama, Despite Due Process Concerns," *Washington Post*, January 1, 2013, http://articles.washingtonpost.com/2013–01–01/world/36323571_1_obama-administration-interrogation-drone-strikes (accessed December 2, 2013).

34. Mark Mazzetti, "Two-Year Manhunt Led to Killing of Al-Alawki in Yemen," *New York Times*, October 1, 2011, www.nytimes.com/2011/10/01/world/middleeast/anwar-al-awlaki-is-killed-in-yemen.html?pagewanted=all&_r=0. (accessed December 1, 2013).

35. A copy of the white paper is available at http://msnbcmedia.msn.com/i/msnbc/sections/news/020413_DOJ_White_Paper.pdf (accessed December 1, 2013).

36. *Ali v. Obama*, Docket No. 11-5103 (D.C. Cir. December 3, 2013) (slip opinion at 23).

37. Steve Vladeck, "D.C. Circuit 1, Guantanamo Bar 0?," 2012, www.lawfareblog.com/2012/06/d-c-circuit-1-guantanamo-bar-0/ (accessed December 6, 2013).

38. Anthony Gregory, *The Power of Habeas Corpus in America: From the King's Prerogative to the War on Terror* (New York: Cambridge University Press for the Independent Institute, 2013).

39. Transcript of oral argument in *Boumediene v. Bush*, T39-14 to 17, www.supremecourt.gov/oral_arguments/argument_transcripts/06–1195.pdf (accessed December 7, 2013).

40. Ibid. at T60-19 to 61-3.

41. Ibid. at T75-6 to 76-11.

42. Ibid. at T41-21 to 25.

43. Transcript of oral argument in *Hamdan v. Rumsfeld*, www.supremecourt.gov/oral_arguments/argument_transcripts/05–184.pdf (accessed December 8, 2013), T57-24 to 58-4.

44. Paul Kahn, *Sacred Violence* (Ann Arbor: University of Michigan Press, 2008), 70.

45. David Luban, "Liberalism, Torture and the Ticking Bomb," *Virginia Law Review* 91 (2005): 1425.

Chapter 8: Conclusion

1. David Strauss, *The Living Constitution* (New York: Oxford University Press, 2010), 8.

2. Ibid., 76.

3. Ibid., 92.

4. Ibid., 99.

5. Akhil Reed Amar, "Rethinking Originalism," *Slate*, September 2005, www.slate.com/articles/news_and_politics/jurisprudence/2005/09/rethinking_originalism.html (accessed December 24, 2013).

6. Strauss, *The Living Constitution*, 95.

7. 539 U.S. 558 (2003).

8. 342 U.S. 165 (1952).

9. 110 U.S. 516 (1884).

10. 110 U.S. 516, 521.

11. Ibid.

12. Ibid., 529.

13. Ibid.

14. Ibid., 530.

15. Ibid., 531.

16. Ibid., 537.

17. Strauss, *The Living Constitution*, 25–26.

18. Ibid., 139.

Bibliography

Books and Articles

Ackerman, Bruce. "The Emergency Constitution." *Yale Law Journal* 113 (2004): 1029–1091.

Amar, Akhil Reed. *America's Constitution: A Biography*. New York: Random House, 2005.

———. *America's Unwritten Constitution: The Precedents and Principles We Live By*. New York: Basic Books, 2012.

———. "Rethinking Originalism." *Slate*, September 2005. http://www.slate.com/articles/news_and_politics/jurisprudence/2005/09/rethinking_originalism.html.

Azmy, Baher. "Executive Detention, *Boumediene* and the New Common Law of Habeas." *Iowa Law Review* 95 (2010): 447–538.

Balkin, Jack, and Sanford Levinson. "Understanding the Constitutional Revolution." *Virginia Law Review* 87 (2001): 1045–1104.

Belknap, Michael. "The Warren Court and Equality." In *Constitutionalism and American Culture: Writing the New Constitutional History*, edited by Sandra F. Van Burkleo, Kermit L. Hall, and Robert J. Kaczorowski, 211–239. Lawrence: University Press of Kansas, 2002.

Bickel, Alexander. *The Supreme Court and the Idea of Progress*. New Haven, CT: Yale University Press, 1978.

Bilder, Mary Sarah. "Colonial Constitutionalism and Constitutional Law." In *Transformations in American Legal History: Essays in Honor of Professor Morton J. Horwitz*, edited by Daniel W. Hamilton and

Alfred L. Brophy, 28–57. Cambridge, MA: Harvard University Press, 2009.

Blackstone, Sir William. *Commentaries on the Law of England*. 4 vols. London, 1809.

Brennan, William. "Why Have a Bill of Rights?" *Valparaiso Law Review* 26 (1991): 1–19.

Chipman Gray, John. "The Nature and Sources of the Law." In *American Legal Realism*, edited by William W. Fisher III, Morton J. Horwitz, and Thomas A. Reed, 34–38. New York: Oxford University Press, 1993.

Corwin, Edward. "The 'Higher Law' Background of American Constitutional Law." *Harvard Law Review* 62 (1928): 149–185.

Dayan, Colin. *The Story of Cruel and Unusual*. Cambridge, MA: Boston Review Press, 2007.

Denbeaux, Mark, and Joshua Denbeaux. *No-Hearing Hearings*. 2006. http://law.shu.edu/publications/guantanamoReports/final_no_hearing_hearings_report.pdf.

Dyer, Justin Buckley. "Slavery and the Magna Carta in the Development of Anglo-American Constitutionalism." *PS: Political Science and Politics* 43 (2010): 479–482.

Dyzenhaus, David. *The Constitution of Law: Legality in a Time of Emergency*. New York: Cambridge University Press, 2006.

Feldman, Noah. *Scorpions: The Battles and Triumphs of FDR's Great Supreme Court Justices*. New York: Twelve, 2010.

Feldman, Stephen. "Diagnosing Power: Postmodernism in Legal Scholarship and Judicial Practice (with an Emphasis on the *Teague* Rule against New Rules in Habeas Corpus Cases)." *Northwestern University Law Review* 88 (1994): 1046–1105.

Fisher, William. "Introduction." In *American Legal Realism*, edited by William W. Fisher, Morton J. Horwitz, and Thomas A. Reed, xi–xvii. New York: Oxford University Press, 1993.

Frank, Jerome. "Law and the Modern Mind." In *American Legal Realism*, edited by William W. Fisher III, Morton J. Horwitz, and Thomas A. Reed, 205–211. New York: Oxford University Press, 1993.

Fraser, Nancy. "Foucault on Modern Power: Empirical Insights and Normative Confusions." *Praxis International* 3 (1981): 272–287.

Freyer, Tony. "Hugo L. Black and the Warren Court in Retrospect." In *The Warren Court in Historical and Political Perspective*, edited by Mark Tushnet, 86–106. Charlottesville: University Press of Virginia, 1993.

Friendly, Henry. "Is Innocence Irrelevant? Collateral Attack on Criminal Judgments." *University of Chicago Law Review* 38 (1970): 142–172.

Gedicks, Frederick. "An Originalist Defense of Substantive Due Process: Magna Carta, Higher Law Constitutionalism, and the Fifth Amendment." *Emory Law Journal* 58 (2009): 585–673.

Gramsci, Antonio. *Selections from the Prison Notebooks*. New York: International Publishers, 1971.

Greenberg, Karen, and Josh Dratel. *The Torture Papers: The Road to Abu Ghraib*. New York: Cambridge University Press, 2005.

Gregory, Anthony. *The Power of Habeas Corpus in America: From the King's Prerogative to the War on Terror*. New York: Cambridge University Press for the Independent Institute, 2013.

Hart, Henry, and Herbert Wechsler. *The Federal Courts and the Federal System*. 2nd ed. Mineola, NY: Foundation Press, 1973.

Hartman, Marshall, and Jeanette Nyden. "Habeas Corpus and the New Federalism after the Antiterrorism and Effective Death Penalty Act of 1996." *John Marshall Law Review* 30 (1997): 337–387.

Hartz, Louis. *The Liberal Tradition in America*. New York: Harcourt Brace Jovanovich, 1955.

Higginbotham, A. Leon. *In the Matter of Color: Race and the American Legal Process*. New York: Oxford University Press, 1978.

Holmes, Oliver Wendell. *The Common Law*. Boston: Little Brown, 1881.

———. "The Path of the Law." In *American Legal Realism*, edited by William W. Fisher III, Morton J. Horwitz, and Thomas A. Reed, 15–24. New York: Oxford University Press, 1993.

Holt, J. C. *Magna Carta*. New York: Cambridge University Press, 1965.

Horwitz, Morton. *The Transformation of American Law, 1780–1860*. Cambridge, MA: Harvard University Press, 1977.

Howard, A. E. Dick. *The Road from Runnymede*. Charlottesville: University of Virginia Press, 1968.

Hutson, James. "The Emergence of the Modern Concept of a Right in America." In *The Nature of Rights at the American Founding and Beyond*, edited by Barry Alan Shain, 25–66. Charlottesville: University Press of Virginia, 2007.

Irons, Peter. *Jim Crow's Children*. New York: Penguin Books, 2003.

Jenks, Edward. "The Myth of Magna Carta." *Independent Review* 4 (1904): 260–273.

Kahn, Paul. *Sacred Violence*. Ann Arbor: University of Michigan Press, 2008.

Kennedy, Duncan. "Freedom and Constraint in Adjudication: A Critical Phenomenology of Judging." *Journal of Legal Education* 36 (1986): 518–562.

——. "The Structure of Blackstone's Commentaries." *Buffalo Law Review* 28 (1979): 208–382.

Konig, David Thomas. "Constitutional Contexts: The Theory of History and the Process of Constitutional Change in Revolutionary America." In *Constitutionalism and American Culture: Writing the New Constitutional History*, edited by Sandra F. Van Burkleo, Kermit L. Hall, and Robert J. Kaczorowski, 3–28. Lawrence: University Press of Kansas. 2002.

Llewellyn, Karl. "A Realistic Jurisprudence—The Next Step." In *American Legal Realism*, edited by William W. Fisher III, Morton J. Horwitz, and Thomas A. Reed, 53–58. New York: Oxford University Press, 1993.

——. "Some Realism about Realism—Responding to Dean Pound." In *American Legal Realism*, edited by William W. Fisher III, Morton J. Horwitz, and Thomas A. Reed, 68–75. New York: Oxford University Press, 1993.

Luban David. "Liberalism, Torture and the Ticking Bomb." *Virginia Law Review* 91 (2005): 1425–1461.

Mayer, Jane. *The Dark Side: How the War on Terror Turned into a War on American Ideals*. New York: Doubleday, 2008.

McCoy, Alfred. *Torture and Impunity*. Madison: University of Wisconsin Press, 2012.

McDowell, Gary. "Coke, Corwin and the Constitution: The 'Higher Law Background' Reconsidered." *Review of Politics* 55 (1993): 393–420.

Michelman, Frank. "Brennan and Democracy." *California Law Review* 86 (1998): 399–427.

Nelson, William. "Byron White: A Liberal of 1960." In *The Warren Court in Historical and Political Perspective*, edited by Mark Tushnet, 139–151. Charlottesville: University Press of Virginia, 1993.

Oliphant, Herman. "Return to Stare Decisis." In *American Legal Realism*, edited by William W. Fisher III, Morton J. Horwitz, and Thomas A. Reed, 199–201. New York: Oxford University Press, 1993.

Pallitto, Robert. *Torture and State Violence in the United States: A Short Documentary History*. Baltimore: Johns Hopkins University Press, 2011.

Pallitto, Robert, and William Weaver. *Presidential Secrecy and the Law*. Baltimore: Johns Hopkins University Press, 2007.

Pound, Roscoe. "The Call for a Realist Jurisprudence." In *American Legal Realism*, edited by William W. Fisher III, Morton J. Horwitz, and Thomas A. Reed, 59–67. New York: Oxford University Press, 1993.

———. "Law in Books and Law in Action." In *American Legal Realism*, edited by William W. Fisher III, Morton J. Horwitz, and Thomas A. Reed, 39–44. New York: Oxford University Press, 1993.

———. "Liberty of Contract." In *American Legal Realism*, edited by William W. Fisher III, Morton J. Horwitz, and Thomas A. Reed, 27–34. New York: Oxford University Press.

Primus, Richard. "Introduction to the Nature of American Rights." In *The Nature of Rights at the American Founding and Beyond*, edited by Barry Alan Shain, 15–24. Charlottesville: University Press of Virginia, 2007.

Purcell, Edward. *Brandeis and the Progressive Constitution*. New Haven, CT: Yale University Press, 2000.

Reid, John Phillip. "The Authority of Rights at the American Founding." In *The Nature of Rights at the American Founding and Beyond*, edited by Barry Alan Shain, 67–115. Charlottesville: University Press of Virginia, 2007.

Scalia, Antonin. "A Dialogue on Statutory and Constitutional Interpretation." *George Washington Law Review* 80 (2012): 1613–1619.

Shapiro, David. "Mr. Justice Rehnquist: A Preliminary View." *Harvard Law Review* 90 (1976): 293–357.

Smith, Rogers. *Civic Ideals: Conflicting Visions of Citizenship in U.S. History*. New Haven, CT: Yale University Press, 1997.

———. *Liberalism and American Constitutional Law*. Cambridge, MA: Harvard University Press, 1985.

Smith, Steven. "The Rehnquist Court and Criminal Procedure." *University of Colorado Law Review* 73 (2002): 1337–1361.

Stoner, James. *Common Law and Liberal Theory*. Lawrence: University Press of Kansas, 1992.

Strauss, David A. *The Living Constitution*. New York: Oxford University Press, 2010.

Streichler, Stuart *Justice Curtis in the Civil War Era: At the Crossroads of American Constitutionalism*. Charlottesville: University Press of Virginia, 2005.

Tushnet, Mark. "The King of France with Forty Thousand Men: *Felker v. Turpin* and the Supreme Court's Deliberative Processes." *University of Chicago Supreme Court Review* 1996 (1996): 163–190.

Urofsky, Melvin. "William O. Douglas as Common Law Judge." In *The Warren Court in Historical and Political Perspective*, edited by Mark Tushnet, 64–85. Charlottesville: University Press of Virginia, 1993.

Vermeule, Adrian. "Common Law Constitutionalism and the Limits of Reason." *Columbia Law Review* 107 (2007): 1482–1532.

Vladeck, Steve. "D.C. Circuit 1, Guantanamo Bar 0?" 2012. www.lawfareblog.com/2012/06/d-c-circuit-1-guantanamo-bar-0/.

Weinberg, Louise. "Federal Common Law." *Northwestern University Law Review* 83 (1989): 805–852.

Wert, James. "With a Little Help from a Friend: Habeas Corpus and the Magna Carta after Runnymede." *PS: Political Science and Politics* 43 (2010): 475–478.

Wiecek, William. *The Sources of Antislavery Constitutionalism*. Ithaca, NY: Cornell University Press, 1977.

Wittes, Benjamin, Robert Chesney, and Larkin Reynolds. *The Emerging Law of Detention 2.0: The Guantanamo Habeas Cases as Lawmaking*. 2012. http://www.brookings.edu/~/media/research/files/reports/2011/5/guantanamo%20wittes/chesney%20full%20text%20update32913.pdf.

Worcester, Kenton. "Editor's Introduction to Magna Carta Symposium." *PS: Political Science and Politics* 43 (2010): 451–456.

Wright, Charles Alan. *The Law of Federal Courts*. 4th ed. St. Paul, MN: West, 1983.

Cases

Ali Ahmed v. Obama, 613 F. Supp. 2d 51 (D.D.C. 2009)

Ali v. Obama, Docket No. 11-5103 (D.C. Cir. December 3, 2013)

The Antelope, 23 U.S. 66 (1825)

Baker v. Carr, 369 U.S. 186 (1961)

Baltimore and Ohio Railroad v. Baugh, 149 U.S. 368 (1893)

Black and White Taxicab and Transfer Co. v. Brown and Yellow Taxicab and Transfer Co., 276 U.S. 518 (1928)

Bob Jones University v. U.S., 461 U.S. 574 (1983)

Boumediene v. Bush, 128 S.Ct. 2229 (2008)

Brecht v. Abramson, 507 U.S. 619 (1993)

Browning-Ferris Industries v. Kelco Disposal, 492 U.S. 257 (1989)

Brown v. Board of Education, 347 U.S. 483 (1954)

City of London v. Wood, 12 Mod. 669, 88 Eng. Rep. 1592 (1702)

Coleman v. Thompson, 501 U.S. 722 (1991)
Commonwealth v. Aves, 41 U.S. 539 (1842)
District Attorney's Office v. Osborne, 557 U.S. 52 (2009)
Dred Scott v. Sandford, 60 U.S. 393 (1857)
Duryea v. Guarnieri, 131 S.Ct. 2488 (2011)
Erie Railroad Co. v. Tompkins, 304 U.S. 64 (1938)
Fay v. Noia, 372 U.S. 391 (1963)
Felker v. Turpin, 518 U.S. 1051 (1996)
Fletcher v. Peck, 10 U.S. 87 (1810)
Gideon v. Wainwright, 372 U.S. 335 (1963)
Griswold v. Connecticut, 381 U.S. 479 (1965)
Hamdan v. Rumsfeld, 548 U.S. 557 (2006)
Hamdi v. Rumsfeld, 542 U.S. 466 (2004)
Harper v. West Virginia, 383 U.S. 663 (1966).
Herrera v. Collins, 506 U.S. 390 (1993)
Hosanna Tabor Evangelical Lutheran Church v. Equal Employment Opportunity Commission, 132 S.Ct. 694 (2012)
Hurtado v. California, 110 U.S. 516 (1884)
Idaho v. Coeur d'Alene Tribe, 581 U.S. 261 (1997)
In re Debs, 158 U.S. 564 (1895)
Kansas v. Colorado, 206 U.S. 46 (1907)
Katzenbach v. Morgan, 384 U.S. 641 (1966)
Keeney v. Tamayo-Reyes, 504 U.S. 1 (1992)
Kent v. Dulles, 357 U.S. 116 (1958)
Klopfer v. North Carolina, 386 U.S. 213 (1966)
Lawrence v. Texas, 539 U.S. 558 (2003)
Lochner v. New York, 198 U.S. 45 (1905)
Mapp v. Ohio, 367 U.S. 643 (1961)
Marbury v. Madison, 5 U.S. 137 (1803)
McLaurin v. Oklahoma State Regents, 339 U.S. 637 (1950)
Miranda v. Arizona, 384 U.S. 436 (1966)
Muller v. Oregon, 208 U.S. 412 (1908)
Murray's Lessee v. Hoboken Land and Improvement Co., 59 U.S. 272 (1856)
The Nereide, 13 U.S. 388 (1815)
Parhat v. Gates, 532 F. 3d 834 (D.C. Cir. 2008)
Plessy v. Ferguson, 163 U.S. 537 (1896)
Prigg v Pennsylvania, 41 U.S. 539 (1842)
Rex v. Allen, 116 Eng. Rep. 179 (1827)
Roberts v. Boston, 59 Mass. 198 (1850)

Rochin v. California, 342 U.S. 165 (1952)
Roe v. Wade, 410 U.S. 113 (1973)
Solem v. Helm, 463 U.S. 277 (1983)
Sommersett v. Stewart, 20 How. 79 (1772)
Southern Pacific Co. v. Jensen, 244 U.S. 205 (1917)
South v. Maryland, 59 U.S. 396 (1855)
Sturges v. Crowninshield, 17 U.S. 122 (1819)
Sweatt v. Painter, 339 U.S. 629 (1950)
Swift v. Tyson, 41 U.S. 1 (1842)
Teague v. Lane, 489 U.S. 288 (1989)
Townsend v. Sain, 372 U.S. 293, 317 (1963)
Trop v. Dulles, 356 U.S. 86 (1958)
U.S. v. Mara, 410 U.S. 19 (1973)
Wolf v. Colorado, 338 U.S. 25 (1949)

Index